Sign Here

The enterprise guide to closing contracts quickly

Alex Hamilton

Praise for *Sign Here*

Even high-end law firms don't have much advice they can offer a competent inhouse lawyer or GC on how to run their contract processes. But Radiant Law is much more than a law firm and Alex is much more than a lawyer. Read this book for insightful, well grounded, incremental, and practical advice on how to solve the Contracting Problem.

– Martin Clausen, former General Counsel of Maersk Line and Managing Director of Syngrato

Alex Hamilton is a compelling voice in contracts. He recognizes that fixing the systemic dysfunction requires establishing new incentives and overhauling the different components of the process. With Sign Here, he guides you through what's required in an insightful and accessible way. It's a unique resource.

– Ken Adams, Author of A Manual of Style For Contract Drafting

Excellent. well written, interesting conceptually and practically. A reminder that for all the lawtech hype we need to understand and engineer the service before we harp on about magic bullets.

– Professor Richard Moorhead

Essential reading for anyone involved in the contracting process - Alex is one of a few genuinely disruptive thinkers in the legal industry.

– Paul Boyle, Group Deputy General Counsel, Serco Plc

Alex shares his experience as a successful transactional lawyer and a master of the contracting process in the best possible way—by breaking down first principles and offering pragmatic, battle-tested solutions.

– Sol Irvine, former General Counsel at Concertiv and Partner, Yuson & Irvine

In my work with general counsel globally, they fall into two categories when thinking about contracts and contract management – where do I begin? or jumping too quickly to fix a small part of the problem. *Sign Here* provides a comprehensive and holistic view of how to assess needs and success in managing and closing contracts, faster. It provides much discipline and practical insight in a field that is crowded with failed attempts.

Duc V. Trang, Managing Director at Major, Lindsey & Africa, former General Counsel and author of Architecture of Deals: Strategies for Transactional Lawyering

In my experience, most attorneys believe that contracting is broken. Unfortunately, they also believe that there is no way to fix it (a comfortable though not helpful posture). Alex's new book colorfully validates the first belief and systematically dismantles the second. This is a must read for anyone who is serious about contracting.

– Michael Naughton, Vice President xMentium, previously Director of Legal Service Innovation at Cisco

First published in Great Britain in 2021.

Alas, reading this book does not make Alex your lawyer.

v 1.0

ISBN 978-1-9196416-1-4

To Vita and Theo

Contents

Introduction

Ten years ago, I did something foolish.

Up to then, I'd had a perfectly normal—bordering on successful—career in law. I'd made partner at a large American firm, was qualified in a couple of jurisdictions, and was known in my specialist area of outsourcing and technology deals... but I had an itch, and it was bothering me.

It seemed to me that there was something deeply wrong with how we were all approaching contracts. It had become a ritualised dance of predictable and often unreasonable positions taken by each side, heated arguments over irrelevant issues, with negotiations driven by "legal" points rather than substance. I was struck by how lawyers' incentives on these deals undermined the process—charging for time wasn't encouraging them to close deals quickly. Meanwhile, business leaders were looking on frustrated as contracts took far too long to complete, while the points they cared about most were being side-lined.

And so, in a moment of madness, I threw that stable career away and started Radiant Law, the first fixed-price law firm specialising in commercial contracts. We not only ditched the timesheet, but we also embraced technology and process improvements, using this as an opportunity to redesign how we delivered legal services.

Over the last ten years, the team at Radiant Law has done more than redesign legal services. With new incentives that encouraged us to get deals signed faster and the opportunity to support the day-to-day contracts of many of the largest companies in the world, we have been busy figuring out how to make contracting fly.

We knew from the beginning that we needed to look beyond the traditional world of contracting. We've worked with Lean[1], data analytics, and technology experts to create a new methodology for transforming contracting processes. The results we've achieved for our clients have been dramatic.

Ten years on, we're ready to share our methodology with you.

Who is this book for?

Every year, companies spend trillions of pounds buying goods and services from other companies. Underpinning every invoice for this spend is a contract. Commercial contracting is a critical capability for every company.

Despite its importance, the typical contracting process tends to be document-centric, slow, and untouched by digitalisation. Companies are haemorrhaging value through mismanagement and racking up costs through unnecessary negotiations.

One of the challenges with contracting well is the number of departments involved and the lack of a clear owner. If ever there was an opportunity to create value at your company, fixing the end-to-end contracting process must be up there as a contender. Whether you're in legal, finance, sales, procurement, or the broader business, in many companies, there is an open goal for the person who steps up and seizes the opportunity to make contracting work better.

This book is for that person. I'm going to show you where you need to start, what the building blocks are, how they fit together, how to

---

[1] Lean is the process improvement approach pioneered by Toyota. Originating in manufacturing, it has since been applied to services and is Radiant Law's core methodology for delivering continuous improvement. As described by our advisor, Professor Norman Faull, "Lean is a system for creating thinking people."

apply automation, and how to introduce a continuous improvement process so your contracting keeps getting better.

Your company will be entering into many different types of contracts, from purchase orders to highly complex transactions. In this book, I will be focusing on the contracts that sit somewhere in the middle, the higher-volume negotiated agreements—your daily deals. Learnings will carry across to contracts at both extremes, but it's the middle that holds the most opportunities for standardisation and improvement.

What this book is not about is contracts themselves. I'm not going to cover how to draft, what should go into your agreement, nor how to negotiate. There won't be any law, and it won't matter where you are based. However, I have included a reading list at the end, which will point you to great resources on these topics.

Why do we have contracts?

Contracts don't look very attractive on your shelf, they don't taste nice, and they won't give you shelter—so what value do they add? The answer is that businesses need to work with others through commercial relationships. And the purpose of the contract is to help get those relationships going.

In other words, the objective of the contracting process is not to create contracts; it's to create and grow relationships. Contracts help us along the way by building confidence. They do this by giving the parties certainty about what the mutual promises are and that those promises will be kept (because there will, at least in theory, be some recourse if they aren't).

But if we're trying to create relationships, why are we so darn'd difficult with each other in negotiations? Why do we keep trying to start abusive relationships? And why are we so focused on what could go wrong rather than on how to make things go right?

How to fix contracting

We need to apply new thinking to fix contracting. We need to start relationships on the right foot. We need to treat contracting as a standardisable process and stop making it up as we go along. We need to recognise that there is no sweeping fix that will make everything alright and that instead, we will have to make lots of small changes to keep improving how we work. We need leaders who will make the process work across our organisations.

Building on these principles, we need to move to a better approach to contracting: RADICAL contracting:

Reasonable rather than maximal positions.

Automated rather than manual processes.

Data-driven rather than relying on folklore.

Incremental improvements rather than large-scale transformations.

Collaborative with the other side and across your organisation rather than adversarial and siloed.

Accelerated rather than ponderous.

Long-term relationships rather than short-term transactions.

I'm going to show you a structured approach to implementing RADICAL contracting using our 3Rs methodology so you can fix your contracting in three stages:

Repeatable: Standardising your contracting process, including putting the core templates and tools in place, ready to be improved.

Robots: Applying cost-effective and straightforward technology that works.

Refinement: Implementing a continuous improvement process that keeps enhancing your contract terms and contracting process to focus on your stakeholders' needs.

There will be lots of different pieces to the puzzle that you will be putting in place at each stage of the 3Rs methodology, and I'm going to walk you through each of these stages step by step:

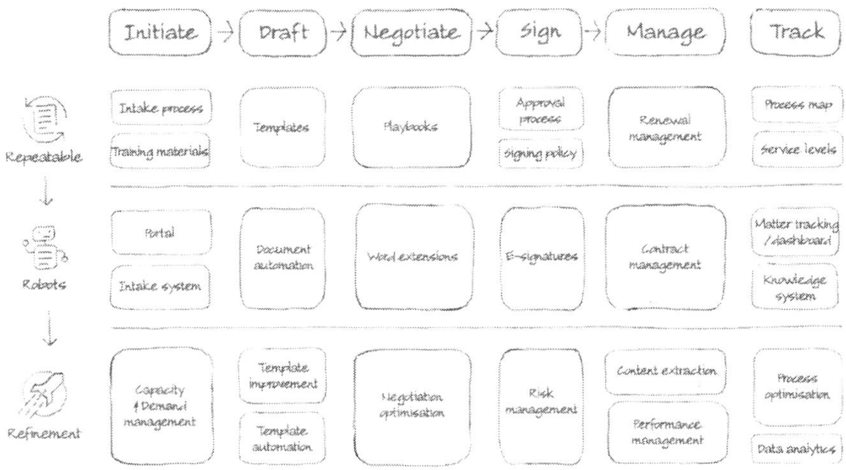

Figure 1 - 3Rs: the full map

The 3Rs methodology will transform your contracting by:

- speeding up your time to close contracts,
- ensuring that you are using the right people to support your contracting,

- reducing your cost-per-contract,
- improving the risk management of your contracting portfolio, and
- delivering better business outcomes from your commercial relationships.

We're moving to an increasingly networked world, where no one company does everything itself for the end consumer. Building an ecosystem of companies around you to help create value will be a core business challenge of the 21st century, so contracting has never been more critical. Now is the time to establish a fantastic contracting process in your company that gives you the relationships and the competitive advantage you need to succeed.

Chapter 1 The Contracting Problem

As a contracting professional, it can be a salutary experience asking a typical business user what they think of the contracting process. From their perspective, contracting is often a hell hole of squabbling over minor points in unreadable documents that costs a fortune and takes forever. They know they need to get through it, but they hate the experience. I call this "the contracting problem".

In this chapter, I will explore the painful reality of contracting and some of its causes. We need to face this if we are going to do better.

Your contracts matter

Contracts matter. To understand why, just consider your company's profit and loss report. You can't send an invoice to a customer without a contract, so all revenue depends on contracts. You also can't get access to power, logistics, IT, or any of the other third-party services your company relies upon without a contract. Without contracts, you would have to build your own power station. Many, if not most, of the lines on your P&L relate to commercial agreements. Your company will inevitably also be partnering with others to achieve common goals.

Think about it from the perspective of your CEO. The typical CEO, according to recent surveys, is probably prioritising: (1) growth, (2) leveraging technology and applying innovation, (3) making savings, (4) environmental, social, and governance issues, (5) dealing with regulatory change, and (6) people and culture. Commercial contracts relate to at least the first five of these six categories, and commercial relationships can often be intrinsic to success.

However, the world of commercial contracts is too often a mess. Why a mess? Let me give you some examples.

Problem 1: Contracts cost too much

World Commerce and Contracting[2] (WorldCC) estimated in 2017[3] that the average company it surveyed was spending almost twice as much as a top-quartile company on getting its contracts in place. They found even a simple and low-risk contract cost, on average, an eye-watering £5,000 to complete for each party, which was almost 40 per cent more expensive than six years earlier.

This is despite legal work having migrated in-house, as law firms priced themselves out of the market. According to a Gartner benchmark in 2018[4], in-house teams review 75 per cent of contracts. The benchmark goes on to offer a clue as to why it costs so much: only 3 per cent of the surveyed legal departments had fully automated their commercial contracts process.

Problem 2: Contracts take too long

We all know the experience of contract processes dragging on. Consider one figure from the Association of Corporate Counsel's 2019 global legal department benchmarking report: the average time to review a contract is over 30 days[5].

The cost of these delays can go far beyond the cost of the contracting process itself. If a sales contract takes a long time to close, revenue is permanently lost, or at the least, cash arrives later.

[2] Formerly called the International Association for Contract & Commercial Management or IACCM.

[3] Or $6,900: https://blog.iaccm.com/commitment-matters-tim-cummins-blog/the-cost-of-a-contract

[4] Gartner's 2018 Legal Technology and Analytics Benchmarking Report.

[5] https://www.acc.com/sites/default/files/2019-06/ACC_Benchmark_062019.pdf

Similarly, if a procurement contract is delayed, the business value is postponed and may even evaporate. Speed is a necessity, not a luxury.

Case Study: The Split Test

In 2018, we helped four companies update their contracts to deal with new privacy legislation that was about to come into effect. We noticed that the four projects were taking wildly different times to complete—some were quick, while others dragged out:

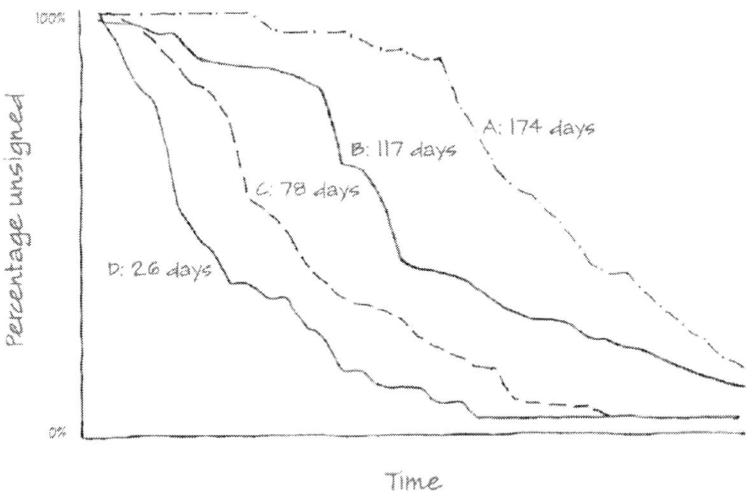

Figure 2 - Burn-down chart of projects

Project D was closing amendments almost seven times faster on average than Project A (26 days on average compared to 174 days).
The range was so surprising that we dug deeper. The team identified two differences between the projects: how good the clients were at getting approvals, signatures, etc. (unsurprisingly, large enterprises struggle) and how reasonable the first draft was (specified by the client). A statistical analysis suggested both factors were affecting the time to complete the projects.

The difference between Project B and Project D stood out. The only difference between the projects was one additional provision asked for by the Project B client to increase the other side's overall liability. That one provision (not required by the change in law) caused the average time to close an amendment to take over four times longer.

Case Study 1 – The Split Test [6]

Problem 3: Contracting hinders rather than helps relationships

Most of your day-to-day contracts will be relational rather than transactional[6]. There will be transactional contracts, too, ranging from simple spot sales to mergers and acquisitions, but the typical business contract covered by this book will start or grow a relationship. Relationships are indeed being created and grown, but successful relationships are often *despite* rather than *because of* the agreement.

Here are three ways this can play out in practice:

- **The contracting process undermines the relationship:** There are many ways to damage a relationship, but common examples include sending out unreasonable and trust-destroying first drafts; adversarial behaviours and use of leverage to maximise outcomes; positional rather than principle-led negotiations that don't maximise the opportunity; and using the contract after signing as a weapon rather than a baseline.

---

[6] A later analysis of fines by the data privacy regulator suggested that the liability change made by the Project B client was pointless. The types of data being processed were low risk and unlikely to be the subject of material fines, even if something went wrong.

[7] There are also "relational" contracts, where companies partner and the relationship is paramount. These contracts tend to fall at the most complex end of the spectrum and hence outside the main scope of this book. There is a resource on relational contracts in the reading list at the end. Hopefully, the developments in that field will be more widely applied across the contracting spectrum.

- **The negotiations focus on the wrong topics**: WorldCC carries out a regular survey of its global members, asking what gets negotiated and what goes wrong in practice[7]. For over a decade, WorldCC has repeatedly found that negotiations focus on what happens when the contract goes completely awry (such as provisions covering liability limits, termination, and indemnities), while what goes wrong in practice is that the parties don't have a common understanding of scope and pricing. All too often, we set up our contracts to fail because we spend our time focusing on failure rather than the basics that would prevent the failure in the first place. It's a true self-fulfilling prophecy.

- **Relationship value leaks:** In another study[8], WorldCC found that companies are, on average, less profitable by over 9 per cent of their revenue because their relationships leak value due to poor contracting practices. We are losing real money by not running our contracts well.

Problem 4: Contracting teams are overstretched

It's not just companies experiencing problems; the contracting teams[9] themselves are suffering.

[7]https://www.worldcc.com/Portals/IACCM/Resources/9934_0_Most%20Negotiated%20Terms%202020.pdf

[8]https://www.worldcc.com/Resources/Content-Hub/View/ArticleId/9773/Poor-Contract-Management-Continues-To-Costs-Companies-9-Of-Their-Bottom-Line

[9] I generally refer to "contracting teams" in this book as they may be organisationally distinct to, or extend beyond, the legal team, but contracting teams usually at least include lawyers. Where I refer to the "business", I mean departments other than the contracting team (but that doesn't mean the contracting team isn't part of the overall business).

- Teams are struggling to deal with the day-to-day demand for contracts, let alone when volumes spike[10]. No wonder the average time to review an agreement is 30 days.

- Meanwhile, general counsels (GCs) are asked to do "more for less". Having delivered the initial saving of moving legal support in-house from expensive law firms, adding more heads is treated with hostility by CFOs[11].

- Contracting teams rarely find the time needed to improve, which is exacerbated by some thinking of change as needing to be transformational and ignoring opportunities for small, quick wins.

The missing pieces

This book contains many of the tools and actions needed to improve your contracting process (and why they matter). Most companies have taken only a few of these steps, which explains many of their problems. We know what happens in practice from collecting data for years through Radiant Law's Contracting Scorecard, a free tool for companies to check how they're doing[12]. This is what the data tells us a typical company has done[13]:

---

10 According to the Radiant Law Contracting Scorecard, 77 per cent of teams have moderate to material slowdowns when there are spikes in volumes.

11 According to Gartner's 2021 Legal Planning & Budgeting report, only 6 per cent of in-house teams were expecting to increase headcount, while 20 per cent were expecting to decrease headcount.

12 https://radiantlaw.com/scorecard

13 The percentages in the notes for this section are based on the responses from 89 companies to Radiant Law's Contracting Scorecard, with the companies ranging from signing at least a hundred contracts a year to many thousands. It is

- Although the company has a contracts-focused legal team, they can't do large, complex deals in-house[14].

- The company has templates for some but not all their common contracts, but they haven't automated them. The templates themselves are generally overly long, unreasonable and unclear[15].

- They've started making materials and training available to the business, but it's haphazard[16].

- The business tends to ask their favourite lawyer for help rather than using a centralised intake process. In any case, there are probably no service levels in place for how fast the contracting team will respond to requests for help (and even if service levels do exist, they are unlikely to be being

---

hard to determine how good the sampling is: it might err towards companies with problems or companies showing off their improvements. However, other data sources, such as the ACC, WorldCC, and Gartner surveys mentioned above, align with the results we are seeing, with all four suggesting that many companies have much room for improvement. There are undoubtedly companies with great contracting processes, but we are seeing only a small proportion in the data who have put most of the steps in place and whose processes are flying.

[14] Although 91 per cent have a contracts legal team, only 31 per cent can handle most strategic deals in-house.

[15] Only 12 per cent have templates for all the contracts that the business could create. 51 per cent have some standard templates for the legal team, but only 11 per cent have unified templates with consistent terms and only 13 per cent have a style guide. 26 per cent have started to automate their templates, but only 4 per cent have automated all their templates.

[16] 79 per cent have run occasional training sessions for the business, but only 11 per cent run a training programme.

measured). Nor are there rules of engagement for requests, with the business often appearing with urgent requests then disappearing for months[17].

- If there is a playbook for negotiation positions, it only covers a few issues and hasn't been updated recently (or goes on for a hundred pages and is unusable)[18].

- Electronic signatures are the one technology that has been introduced somewhere in the organisation, but not for all contracts[19].

- The company either stores its contracts in an online folder or in a contract management system with haphazard data. It will often not be able to lay its hands on a signed version or know whether it has been amended[20].

- The contracting process will be being tracked manually, if at all, with little data and no analysis. The contracting team often can't tell you how many contracts they are supporting each year[21].

---

[17] 56 per cent have not put in place a central place to send requests. 32 per cent have service levels for responding but only 11 per cent track whether they are meeting the service level.

[18] 51 per cent have playbooks, but only 11 per cent consider theirs to be comprehensive and regularly updated.

[19] Only 21 per cent are using electronic signatures for all their contracts.

[20] 47 per cent use a contract management system, but only 19 per cent systematically track metadata and 20 per cent proactively manage contract performance.

[21] Only 25 per cent consistently track progress of matters, 16 per cent use a

- The contracting team will also be overstretched, only able to get to improvements haphazardly[22].

In short, the typical company is light on tools, technology, data, and process.

When we talk to teams about their progress, they regularly tell us they fear they're behind their peers at other companies. The good news is that they are often not behind; the bad news is it's because so many of their peers are doing poorly.

Three perverse incentives

"*Never, ever think about anything else when you should be thinking about the power of incentives.*" – Charlie Munger

Some particularly perverse incentives are worth bearing in mind as you try to fix your contracting processes:

Protecting relevance

You may have noticed that some participants seem to make things more complicated than they should be. They may also appear to squirrel away knowledge. This behaviour often stems from a fear that their job will be at risk if everyone finds out that their part in the process isn't exactly rocket science.

Interestingly, participants are often quick to point out that the person's role down the corridor is blindingly simple, whereas theirs

---

tracking system (as opposed to a shared document).

[22] Only 13 per cent are running an ongoing improvement programme (as opposed to ad hoc efforts), and only 4 per cent are using data to inform that programme.

is particularly hard. Funnily enough, if you ask the other person, they might have a similar perspective, except that it's their role that's particularly hard.

Let's be honest: except for a few tricky types of deals, there's nothing associated with the contracting process that's that complicated. The law isn't so hard; any of the points that come up are perfectly understandable by a moderately bright participant. Even the technology involved is rather banal (as we'll see later, it's mainly just databases, workflow, and document transformations).

What's hard is cutting through all the noise to make things simple. If you see someone creating a ton of complexity, they're not doing a great job. You may need to reassure them that they will still have a job if they help make the process go faster, not slower.

The good news is that anyone adept at simplifying things will be precious to their employer. The even better news for experienced team members is that if they can make the work more straightforward, it can be supported by more junior team members or suppliers, freeing them up to work on the more strategic and exciting deals.

Playing safe

Your average CEO doesn't wake up every morning wondering how to crush all risk out of existence. They're often looking for chances to take on more risk in a clever way as they try to grow the company and take advantage of opportunities.

But by the time you get down to the line workers, the overriding concern is often to avoid being accused later of missing something or doing something wrong. This tendency shows itself in the unreasonable standard templates that companies too often use and how they behave in negotiations.

Some business cultures have finger-pointing far too embedded to expect participants to act in any other way. In others, though, it's a question of whether leaders will provide support.

Clocking up hours

Not entirely unconnected to the above is the billable hour's impact, which is one of the most effective ways to get intelligent people to play dumb. Unfortunately, this system is deeply entrenched in most law firms.

The billable hour drives up complexity and slows down transactions. Why send a reasonable draft when you can send something one-sided that will inspire an unreasonable response and hence increase the time spent battling back to some middle ground? Why simplify processes if you can't charge as much? And why use automation that gets rid of billable hours?

At Radiant Law, we know that if a law firm is involved on the other side of a negotiation, it will take three to five times longer to settle a contract than when it's an in-house team (who aren't incentivised to drag the matter out). We avoided timesheets from day one because we knew they would incentivise team members to make things more complicated. By only charging on a fixed-price basis, we were instead incentivised to speed up our clients' contracts.

The easy solution to this problem is to stop buying time from your law firm and ensure that they aren't incentivising the people working on your deals to make them overly complex. It's incredible how behaviours will change when you fix this[23].

---

[23] Unfortunately, even when billable hour incentives aren't in play, lawyers (whether external or internal) do tend to make things more complex than necessary. Getting rid of the billable hour helps but doesn't solve everything.

Summary

Contracting excellence is becoming increasingly critical to business success, but generally, we aren't doing it well. Contracts typically take too long and cost too much to put in place, and the contracting process and contracts themselves are too often not setting organisations up for relationship success. The teams responsible for the contracting process tend to be overstretched and struggling to implement change while facing ongoing budgetary pressures.

In practice, though, most teams haven't put in place many of the basics that can help solve these issues. Meanwhile, perverse incentives, such as fears of redundancy and finger-pointing, and the billable hour are hindering progress.

The good news is that all of this is fixable and there is a better way. Some ground-breaking companies have figured out how to increase productivity, reduce costs, speed up the contracting process, and create happy customers and suppliers, as well as a happy contracting team. Time to find out how they do that.

Chapter 2 Rethinking Contracting

The problems in the contracting process can feel so embedded that change seems impossible. Change is possible, but you need to apply new thinking to the issues.

In this chapter, I'm going to explore four principles that are crucial to delivering a better contracting process:

- contracting should foster great relationships,
- contracting is a standardisable process,
- there is no silver bullet, and
- fixing contracting requires leadership.

Building on these fundamental principles, I will then introduce the RADICAL approach to contracting and the 3Rs improvement methodology.

Principle 1: Contracting should foster great relationships

"Contract law is essentially a defensive scorched-earth battleground where the constant question is, 'if my business partner was possessed by a brain-eating monster from beyond spacetime tomorrow, what is the worst thing they could do to me?'" - Charles Stross

In the previous chapter, I talked about how contracting can hinder the relationships it should be underpinning. Now let's turn it on its head and consider how contracting can help:

- we can send reasonable first drafts (discussed further below),

- we can focus the contract discussions on what is essential to successful delivery instead of concentrating on liability if it goes wrong,

- we can adopt principle-led negotiations, as argued for in Fisher, Ury, and Patton's brilliant book Getting to Yes and try to grow the outcome for both parties, and

- we can actively manage the relationship by using the contract as a baseline and recognising that the deal will need to evolve.

Principle 2: Contracting is a standardisable process

"*If you can't describe what you are doing as a process, you don't know what you're doing.*" - W. Edwards Deming

Every deal is different, but the question to ask is how different? Traditionally, contracting has been handled in a somewhat haphazard manner, emphasising bespoke agreements and a process that is more art than science. But if you take a step back and look at the bigger picture, there is a natural sequence to what needs to be done, which people generally follow. Do it long enough, and you'll know what issues are likely to come up. Yes, there will always be outlier deals where everything breaks down, and the other side manages to turn what should take a few days or weeks into many months of hell, but these are the exception, not the rule[24].

If we focus on standardising the "happy path", as programmers call it, and treat the "deals gone bad" as the exception and not the norm[25], then we have a chance to make progress.

[24] In our experience, these account for less than 10 per cent of small to medium-sized deals if you start with reasonable terms.

Many advantages come from standardisation:

it's easier to teach the process to more junior members of your team and develop their skills if you have a clear and well-documented approach,

you'll reduce variability, helping make the process cheaper and faster while increasing quality and predictability[26],

your team will have to spend less time on the mechanical parts (and the mechanical parts will be more readily automated), making the work more engaging and your team more productive, and

only once things are standardised can you start systematically improving them.

This last point is crucial. It's when you have a single, documented way of working that you have a baseline from which to make improvements.

Another aspect of standardisation is recognising that contracting is a well-understood discipline. Although many companies haven't finished putting the basics in place, the things you need to do and what works are predictable, and I spell them out in this book. You also don't need to reinvent the wheel. You will need to make standard solutions work for your circumstances, but generally, your approach will have strong similarities with other high-performing companies. "Happy families are all alike," as Tolstoy observed.

---

[25] Deals gone bad are, however, an excellent source of learning for how to improve the process and minimise their occurrence in the future.

[26] Reducing variability is a core concept in applying Lean to improve outcomes. For more on standardising work (and the connected need to level work), see the books in the reading list on Lean.

Principle 3: There is no silver bullet

"Of all the monsters who fill the nightmares of our folklore, none terrify more than werewolves because they transform unexpectedly from the familiar into horrors. For those, we seek bullets of silver that can magically lay them to rest." – Frederick P. Brooks Jr.[27]

Contrary to the enthusiastic presentations from legal tech providers that you have no doubt seen, there is, alas, no single system or improvement that will solve all your contracting issues. Why is this?

- We are dealing with messy humans and all their emotions and needs. However neatly we want them to fit into a perfectly automated system, it's never that simple.

- We are also dealing with the vast complexity of the real world, where commercial contracts bite. As much as we want to describe the world with taxonomies and pre-set options, exceptions always appear in practice.

- As I describe in this book, there are many aspects to improving contracting. Trying to solve them all in one swoop would mean taking on a complex, risky and expensive transformation, even with the improbable assumption of having sufficient information about what will work in advance.

---

[27] From Frederick P. Brooks Jr's brilliant essay "No Silver Bullet – Essence and Accident in Software Engineering" where he argued in 1987 that there was no single development in either technology or management technique that could transform productivity, reliability, or simplicity in software development within a decade.
http://worrydream.com/refs/Brooks-NoSilverBullet.pdf

So, while it is very human and understandable to wish it weren't so, there is no silver bullet that will solve everything. This is true of contract lifecycle management software, which was the rebranding that marketing departments at software companies came up with when adding features to cover each contracting process stage. This is true of artificial intelligence, which is still limited to small parts of the contracting process without any progress on systems that truly understand contracts' content. This is true of the blockchain, which has little to add to contracts that a database couldn't better handle. This is true of robotic process automation (RPA), a way of gluing together antiquated systems. And it's true of anything labelled "next generation".

Instead of a silver bullet, think in terms of a silver shotgun cartridge (or shell)—make lots of small changes rather than one big change. Try something, see if it works, embrace it if it does, and repeat.

You might find it depressing to discover that there is no single solution and that what you suspected to be snake oil is snake oil, but there is good news here, too: because many changes can be made as relatively small tweaks, they can also be cheap, fast, and low risk.

Principle 4: Fixing contracting requires leadership and a team

"Leadership is not a position or a title, it is action and example." – Donald McGannon.

Contracting is a highly cross-functional activity (or at least it should be). Just within one party, and even for a more straightforward contract, you could have sales or procurement, operations, finance, regulatory, and possibly other specialist departments involved. This raises a couple of challenges:

- First, contracting is inherently more complicated to fix than a process contained within one department. Often, hand-offs are messy, responsibilities are not clearly defined, and the list of stakeholders is vague.

- Second, you probably won't find a chief contracts officer in the C-suite, so who is the contracting process leader in your organisation?

It is common, especially in larger companies, for participants to stick to their part of the contract, with no one leading the improvement of the overall process. But this is a missed opportunity. For the bold, there is a real chance to add demonstrable business value by stepping up.

Leadership is required to create a functioning and coherent end-to-end process. It would be best, though, to err on the side of collaboration and coordination rather than command and control, and anyone proposing to do this would do well to get their own house in order first.

Leadership is also nothing without a team. You will not only need to bring others with you, but you will also need access to a wide range of skills. No one person in your organisation is likely to have all the skills necessary to truly fix contracting, especially given all the disciplines that turn out to be so relevant, such as legal, design, project management, data analytics, process improvement, and so on.

There are, however, many ways to get access to these skills, including in the nascent legal operations corners of larger legal teams and from third-party suppliers (especially the less traditional ones) and other departments within your organisation.

I also believe that participants in the process, including the lawyers, could learn new skills if they were, heaven forbid, to read broadly. This view, sometimes espoused as the "T-shaped"[28] professional, suggests that although you need to bring a core expertise to sit at the table (the vertical stroke of the T), you add more value through a broader but shallower understanding of many other topics (the horizontal stroke). If a little knowledge is a dangerous thing, then just read more! It's probably easier for someone with a deep understanding of the contracting process to learn other skills than for an expert in another discipline to absorb the nuances of contracting.

Introducing RADICAL contracting

Building on these principles (focusing on creating great relationships, standardising the process, accepting there are no silver bullets, and recognising the need for leadership and a team) brings us to Radiant Law's approach: RADICAL contracting. At its heart, RADICAL contracting focuses on creating quick, simple processes that prioritise what matters, relies on empiricism rather than opinion for improvements, and seeks to achieve good enough results with the other side to allow the relationship to get going.

Here is a summary of how RADICAL contracting compares to the traditional approach to contracting:

Traditional approach	RADICAL approach
Maximal positions	Reasonable positions
Manual	Automated
Folklore	Data-driven

[28] There are other variations of this idea, including O-shaped and Delta-shaped lawyers. See https://www.oshapedlawyer.com/ and https://www.legalexecutiveinstitute.com/delta-model-personal-effectiveness-skills/

Big bang or stasis	Improving iteratively
Adversarial	Collaborative
Ponderous	Accelerated
Transactional relationships	Long-term relationships

Reasonable positions

Companies often adopt a maximalist approach in their contracts, trying to win as much as possible on every point rather than being reasonable and heading straight to the middle ground. This might be appropriate for the most critical points in the deal (anchoring can work[29]), but I consider this a fundamental mistake when applied generally across the contract:

- **Speed to close**: Unreasonable terms create negotiations that slow down signing the agreement, reducing its value.

- **Losing deals**: Unreasonable terms can even kill deals. The other side may engage to see if you are serious, but if you continue to insist on your positions, they might walk away[30].

---

[29] Anchoring is when you make the first offer in a negotiation, which has been shown by psychologists Daniel Kahneman and Amos Tversky to tend to change the behaviour of the other side and pull them towards the initial offer. See these Harvard articles for more on the topic:
https://www.pon.harvard.edu/tag/anchoring-in-negotiation/

[30] Case in point: when writing this book, I planned to use a publishing house that claimed publicly to have highly reasonable terms. When they sent the actual contract, this turned out not to be the case, and when asked to change the most egregious points, they refused. I turned to Kindle Direct Publishing (Amazon has been busy disrupting the publishing industry) and a brilliant team of helpers found through Upwork. Unreasonable contracts can have real-world effects.

- **Winning the wrong points:** Unreasonable positions on topics that are not central to the contract yield little value.

- **Long-term deals need to be reasonable:** For a long-term relationship to work, both sides need to feel good about the negotiation outcome long after it has been signed.

- **Inviting retaliation:** Even if you are the overwhelmingly dominant partner, you still need the other side to cooperate over the long term, as there will often be opportunities for retaliation.

Unreasonable starting positions beget unreasonable responses. In contrast, the response to reasonable terms is typically just to accept them or raise minor points (although that's especially the case if you have an in-house lawyer on the other side[31]). In any event, you can always say no to unreasonable responses and hold your ground, so even if you get an unusually unreasonable reaction, it doesn't mean that you must go backwards.

The model we espouse is sending out terms that you would be OK signing as-is if you were on the other side. Reasonable positions represent the likely outcome if two well-advised parties hammered out a compromise that they could both live with. This is far from "giving the farm away", and the positions should reflect both your needs and those of the other side.

---

[31] As mentioned in Chapter 1, our experience is that deals involving an external law firm will, on average, take three to five times longer to close. The delay is particularly exacerbated when the external lawyer doesn't regularly negotiate the relevant type of contract. The counterexample is that a highly experienced external lawyer is more likely to focus on what matters and cut to the chase—you just don't see them often in day-to-day deals.

I acknowledge this approach is controversial because it requires giving up potential gains that would come if the other side capitulated. My argument is that these potential gains are generally not that valuable in practice. The value of closing contracts quicker and getting going earlier more often outweighs possible gains from protracted negotiations[32]. I have also frequently seen what happens when one-sided terms are put in place, driving defensive behaviour by the weaker side that destroys value. We have also seen high-profile examples where onerous terms failed to guarantee delivery (for example, the famous £10 billion disaster with the National Health Service's IT contracts in the early 2000s).[33]

---

[32] Try to identify how many times your company has had material disputes about its contracts in the past ten years and, of those disputes, how many turned on the nuance of a particular clause. We ask this regularly of clients, and they have consistently had so few examples (most often none) that it has been impossible to use the data to build statistical models of contractual risk (even if the potential impact is large, likelihood tends to 0). I believe the absence of data, like the dog that didn't bark in the Sherlock Holmes' story, is telling. The usual estimates that are bandied around is that far fewer than 1 per cent of deals end up in material disputes.

If this doesn't land for you, consider how likely it is that an issue arises where you would be protected with an unreasonable position, but not with a reasonable position (which, by definition, seeks to address both party's legitimate concerns). Then consider the cost of winning that position compared to the value of having your contracts start faster.

My experience is that we are almost always surprised by what topics come up in disputes (they would have been fully locked down if we knew they were going to be an issue in advance). Better to focus on making sure that it is clear what is going to be done each month and going to be paid. Those tend to be the points that matter in practice and that you can address in advance.

[33] https://www.henricodolfing.com/2019/01/case-study-10-billion-it-disaster.html

A final point, if you still need persuading: although it's yet to be generally acknowledged by the contracting industry, environmental, social, and governance (ESG) issues are firmly and permanently on the corporate board agenda. How a company interacts with its suppliers, customers and partners is part of the social aspect of ESG. Unreasonable-going-on-abusive terms and behaviours often used by dominant parties raise real ESG issues and are probably at odds with what their boards claim to care about.

Case Study: The Negotiation

A large customer wanted to buy a software-as-a-service product from a small supplier. There was significant business value for the customer once it got the product up and running. Although the product was standard and working with many other customers, the customer needed some minor changes that would take one month to complete.

The customer sent its standard terms, which were unreasonable, and the supplier pushed back. Negotiations dragged on for six months, but eventually, the parties reached a compromise and signed the deal. Despite the negotiations, the supplier had taken on liability far above the value of the contract.

The supplier made sure to spell out the customer's dependencies in the contract to manage the risk. The customer treated this as a transaction and under-resourced the team delivering the dependencies. The customer consequently was responsible for the few delivery delays (the supplier carefully managed the change process given the contract's risks). The supplier delivered the changes in two months from the date of signature with no liability. The project was six months late, and the customer lost significant business value.

The customer's lawyers undoubtedly congratulated themselves on having locked the supplier into a robust contract that ensured delivery. Meanwhile, angels wept.

Case Study 2 - The Negotiation

Automated

I have a complicated relationship with technology. I have been fascinated with it since saving up for a computer at 10, I talk about it regularly at conferences, and we are keen creators and users of it at Radiant Law. But I am also sceptical that everything can and should be automated, especially given contracting is about creating relationships between humans. At the same time, there is no glory or value in carrying out manually the simple and repetitive tasks that a computer can do just as well, if not better.

When it comes to automation, I look to Toyota's approach. Rather than automate complicated processes with sophisticated robots, they first make the process as lean as possible and then apply automation when they hit constraints on further improvements[34]. There is now a rich ecosystem of contracting technology, and some of it really does help. I'm going to devote a significant portion of this book to exploring this area and identifying the systems that give you the most bang for your buck, but core to the RADICAL approach is that you start with getting your processes and basics in order before applying automation. Once you've done that, automate all the parts that you sensibly can.

Data-driven

The contracting world is not short of opinions. As a young lawyer, a long list of rules was beaten into me about what matters and what to do. It's not that these rules are necessarily incorrect, but on reflection, many are arbitrary and few, if any, are informed by data. Firmly held convictions are not the same as objective truth.

---

[34] Which doesn't mean that Toyota builds new factories with no automation. There are known solutions that work. They do, however, have a bias towards technology that can be repurposed as they learn.

If we are going to make progress, we need to measure things that matter and put our beliefs to the test. We need to experiment and be prepared to fail. Almost five hundred years after the start of the scientific revolution, it is time that we embrace empiricism and move beyond handed-down folklore.

Data can be quick and easy to collect, can tell us whether the adjustments we are making are helping, and can be a powerful way to change behaviours. After all, there is nothing quite as compelling as numbers. It's time to ditch the fairy tales and find out what works.

Iterative improvements

We've established that there are no silver bullets, but our approach goes further: to avoid transformations as much as possible. Improving contracting is a grind. You need to keep tweaking and learning, and you want to do this as quickly and safely as possible. Try to use small steps with tight feedback loops that are achievable in days or, even better, a few hours. We try to avoid projects that take more than a couple of weeks to deliver as they are probably being over-engineered. You can implement most of the individual actions suggested in this book in that time frame.

Let go of your inner perfectionist for the first version! Try to adopt an approach of getting something—anything—going and improving it from there. Until you use something in practice, it is adding no value. Only when you use it will you understand what works and what doesn't. Pursue perfection in your processes[35] but recognise that you will never achieve it. There is always *something* you can improve.

[35] Perfection is the goal (that is, of course, never reached) of process improvement, but this is not the same as lawyer perfectionism, which can, for example, result in rounds and rounds of drafting tweaks that add little value.

Avoiding a big-bang approach to change is generally a good thing: small changes are easier to get going, lower risk, are more agile, and let you deliver value faster. You may still need transformation projects, but you can make even these relatively small, lightweight, and quick. And it doesn't mean you should make the changes randomly. There is an inherent logic in the sequence, which I describe in this book[36].

Collaborative

I talked about the need to connect the departments within your organisation and the overall goal of great commercial relationships with the other parties. Collaboration[37] is core to our approach.

---

[36] As noted by one commenter on this book, Lean can involve radical changes as well as ongoing iterative changes, and there is a tension between me arguing for a RADICAL change while espousing iterative changes. Both fair points. My perspective is that there needs to be a transformational change in the mindset around contracting, but teams should err on the side of small, quick changes in implementation, as large IT transformation projects, in particular, have so often had a poor pay-off. Although people don't like discussing failures publicly (we have heard plenty of horror stories off the record), there's a clue in all the articles on the internet about how to avoid the mistakes of the past with contract lifecycle management and how it will be different this time. For more on radical change in Lean, see: http://leanmagazine.net/agile/kaikaku-mind-the-concept-of-radical-change/

[37] Professor Ian Macneil, a founder of the relational approach to contract law, considered cooperation to be at the heart of all relational agreements (and argued that the vast majority of contracts have a relationship component and are not just transactional): "The word 'solidarity' (or 'trust') is not inappropriate to describe this web of interdependence, externally reinforced as well as self-supporting, and expected future co-operation. The most important aspect of solidarity … is the extent to which it produces similarity of selfish interests, whereby what increases (decreases) the utility of one participant also increases (decreases) the utility of the other … Seldom, if ever, is this merger of interests complete, but it is omnipresent, immensely significant, and, in a vast range of circumstances, complete for most practical purposes … [S]imilarity of interests may be produced

Playing nicely within your organisation is obvious; playing nicely with the other side, less so. I've talked about the reasonableness aspect to contracting, but it goes further. The overall experience we create for the other side is intrinsic to building confidence and trust and maximising opportunities to generate value. Therefore, the other side is a crucial stakeholder in your process, and the way you engage with them is critical to success.

It means that contracting teams that refuse to engage with the other side are doing their organisation a disservice. It means that we should negotiate in an open way to maximise the pie's overall size and not just our part of it. And it means that we should approach each discussion with an open mind as to what the best outcome might be.

Accelerated

Speed in contracting is achievable, and nothing is inevitable about the ponderous pace of traditional contracting. I gave you an example in the case study in Chapter 1, where one company was seven times faster than another in closing its contracts. In Chapter 8, I will show you how you can knock 85 per cent off the typical time to close a deal.

My point with putting "accelerated" at the heart of the RADICAL approach is the importance of reducing time to close[38]. Don't worry. Even with vastly faster contracting, you still have time to

---

by external forces such as sovereign law. But ... solidarity may and does arise internally in relations." – Economic Analysis of Contractual Relations: Its Shortfalls and the Need for a "Rich Classificatory Apparatus", 75 Northwestern University Law Review 1034.

[38] There are also times when a speedy contracting process is not in your interest, and you can always slow those deals down. The point is to have the option.

explore options and think through the consequences. Those are things worth spending time on. It's the activities that generally soak up time that can be cut back.

Long-term relationships

The objective of your contracting process should be to err on the side of creating long-term rather than transactional relationships. However much we speed up contracting, it will still cost money. If you invest in the relationship, you will be incurring more costs; if you don't, you will be reducing potential value. It's too expensive and wasteful to churn through customers and suppliers, so long-term relationships are valuable[39].

Having a long-term goal means you won't know exactly how it will end up at the point you sign. Therefore, you need to create enough confidence through contracting to let the relationship get going and create enough structure to help you keep growing that relationship. So, flexible contracting arrangements and investment in contract performance management are essential. It also means that win-win is more than a nice-to-have.

---

[39] There are also times when transactional is good enough and maximalist positioning might be the right move. Again, the point is to have the option and to err towards building relationships.

Case Study: Relationships First

An in-house lawyer reviewed the contractual disputes at their company to see what changed after the company created its internal legal team and started legal reviews of contracts. They couldn't find any change to the already low number of disputes.

They concluded that the company's long-running focus on building relationships with counterparties was more important than legal reviews.

Case Study 3 - Relationships First

The 3Rs methodology

If you want your contracting to be RADICAL, the obvious questions are: how do we deliver it, and what should come first? This takes us to the 3Rs methodology for implementing RADICAL contracting: Repeatable, Robots, and Refinement.

Figure 3 – Repeatable, Robots, Refinement

Underpinning the 3Rs methodology is a crucial observation: contracting is well understood, and you can follow a path that others have created as everyone needs the same essential components. In other words, there is a logical sequence to the changes you want to put in place:

Repeatable: First, put in place the basic tools that can be improved over time, such as contract templates, playbooks, and standard processes. These don't require any automation; in fact, they need to exist before you can start to apply technology.

Robots: Once you have the basics in place, you can introduce technology—in particular, simple technology that includes, where possible, systems already in use within your company. The technology may not end up being the final system but look for quick wins that mean you can get immediate benefits and set yourself up for a continuous improvements approach.

Refinement: Once you have the foundations, you can implement a continuous improvement process driven by stakeholder needs and draw on diverse disciplines, such as Lean, design, and data analytics. In this stage, you will keep getting better, but you will never be done. Perfection will remain elusive, but you'll be able to demonstrate business value, and quality and cost-effectiveness can keep improving at the speed the business needs.

Summary

To fix contracting, we need to think differently. In this chapter, I highlighted the importance of contracts in creating commercial relationships, how you must standardise your processes to improve them, how there are no silver bullets that will fix everything, and the need and opportunity for leadership. Building on these, I introduced the RADICAL approach to contracting: **R**easonable terms, **A**utomated, **D**ata-driven, **I**ncremental improvements, **C**ollaborative, and **A**ccelerated to create **L**ong-term relationships.

We are now going to dive into the 3Rs methodology: Repeatable, Robots, and Refinement. In the following six chapters, I will look at each stage, with an introductory chapter on fundamental principles and a subsequent chapter talking through the core improvement activities. I will describe these improvement activities using a pattern (problem, solution, and points to consider) that echoes the pattern language invented by the architect Christopher Alexander[40] and adopted by the software world. There is so much we can learn from outside law!

[40] See the book A Pattern Language: Towns, Buildings, Construction by Christopher Alexander.

Chapter 3 Repeatable: Core Principles

The Repeatable stage is about getting the basics in place before thinking about automation. In this chapter, I'm going to cover the fundamental principles that will underpin these basics:

- a framework for the different stages in the contracting process,
- how to approach implementing change in a way that sticks,
- how to make knowledge explicit so that everyone in the team can benefit,
- who should be doing your contracting,
- how to build an ecosystem of suppliers, and
- the implications of whether you start with your template.

The contracting process

"*All models are wrong, but some are useful.*" - George Box

At the heart of the Repeatable stage is the principle that we can standardise contracting and have a consistent process for handling contracts of a particular type.

I am going to be following a generic set of high-level stages for the contracting process.

Figure 4 - Stages of a deal

- **Initiate**: This covers the start of the deal when the basic principles are being agreed. In sales, this would run from leads through to an almost-closed opportunity. In procurement, this would include needs recognition and early stages, such as requests for information and proposals. When the procurement process involves competition, that will also fall into the drafting and negotiation stages. From the contracting team's perspective, "initiate" covers the intake process when the team is engaged for assistance and starts collecting information on what is needed.

- **Draft**: This covers the creation of the first draft of the contract. Although there will be ongoing drafting as part of the negotiation of the contract terms, I have made generating the first draft a distinct stage because much of the legal tech for drafting treats the process as a one-off event (afterwards, it usually becomes redline in Word).

- **Negotiate**: This covers the in-depth negotiations of the contract. Although it appears after drafting, there will often have been at least commercial-level discussions before the drafting stage. If the other side created the first draft of the contract, this stage would also include your review of that draft.

- **Sign**: This covers signing the actual agreement and the approvals process.

- **Manage**: Once the contract is signed, the relationship needs to be maintained. This stage covers the hand-over and operationalising of the agreement and the contractual relationship management, including future changes and extensions and any eventual termination.

There are a couple of things to bear in mind about this model.

First, it's pretty legal-centric and errs towards higher volume contracting. Procurement might describe the drafting and negotiation stages as just one step in their model of the process. Sales would probably mutter something about "papering the deal". These are fair points, but I have split the process up like this because:

- it enables us to reason about both sales and procurement contracting processes at the same time,
- it helps make sense of the legal tech market, and
- these are the main steps for turning a vague consensus into a legally enforceable contract.

Second, much of the value from the commercial relationship is created in the initiation and management steps. It's how you select your partners, nurture the relationship, and create value for one another that will drive success. The contracting process can add clarity, increase trust, and give you the confidence to get going, but it's just part of a bigger picture. And that's the heart of the RADICAL approach: we need contracts, but it's not all about the contracts.

Implementing change

During all the stages of the 3Rs, you will be implementing new tools and systems. Therefore, now is the time to consider how best to approach these projects and build your organisational change muscles.

The most critical part of the Repeatable stage is making sure that the contracting team uses the same process and approach. If this isn't the norm yet in your organisation, it can come as a big shock to the team members. However, it's an inevitable part of maturing and reflects the necessary mindset of improving together rather than operating as islands. Making a change as an individual is far less valuable than making a change as a team. If you can't spread improvements through the team, they will have little impact and likely die off.

The key to making effective change is avoiding perfectionism, which can be challenging for lawyers! Making something better, getting it used, and then coming back and improving it again later is far more valuable than working on it until it's "perfect"[41].

Similarly, you'll want to adopt the Pareto Principle, which says that 80 per cent of the value will come from 20 per cent of the effort. Avoiding completionism, as well as perfectionism, is essential. It's much better to get a simple tool in place to cover at least one common-use case and then extend it once it is being used. That way, you'll have an idea of what matters in practice, which will often be very different from what you might have thought beforehand.

Overall, I urge you to adopt an approach of prioritising action over discussion and, if in doubt, just do it. There's no need for projects

---

[41] This argument may be counter-intuitive for readers with legal training. We have had it drummed into us that we must get it right, that spending more time will lead to better outcomes, and that we have to avoid being open to being second guessed in the future. Process improvement thinking brings a different perspective: we only know when something will work by identifying a metric and then trying out the "improvement" and seeing whether the metric gets better. For more on applying empiricism to improvement, see these articles on the plan-do-check/study-act cycle (PDCA or PDSA):
https://www.thinkleansixsigma.com/article/pdca-cycle and
https://www.process.st/deming-cycle/

to improve contract templates to take six months. They can be improved in mere weeks and then improved again later.

Here are some principles for how to approach implementing change:

- **Momentum:** Starting with small wins and building an ethos of continuous improvement will help set up a context in which more ambitious projects can be rolled out.
- **Have a plan and a budget:** You need a plan for rolling out improvements and to make someone accountable for delivery. That person needs to be empowered and publicly supported from the top. You need to budget not only for the initial activity or system but also for the implementation and training costs. Implementation costs can be high—in some cases, they're more than the cost of the system itself.
- **Sell the benefits**: You need to sell the benefits, not just to the organisation but also to team members. Communication throughout the project is essential. The basic rule is that you cannot over-communicate.
- **Minimise the pain**: You should select and implement the project in a way that makes the personal process of change as easy as possible. Use pilots and testing, and knock the edges off before rolling it out widely.
- **Champions and beachheads**: Get going with champions first to ensure that you can demonstrate a fully working tool or system before a wider roll-out. Find enthusiasts who look for potential (rather than problems) to be your champions.
- **Training:** Training is usually essential, but it doesn't necessarily have to be done by external providers.

Enthusiastic champions are often the best people to train the rest of the team.

- **Finally, pick up the sceptics**: Once the new system or tool is in place and working, you can address the sceptics and do what you need to do to get them using it. Sceptics bring a lot of value, too. They will ask the hard questions and force the rigour that will be needed in the long run.

- **Persistence**: There will be setbacks, and not everyone will leap at the opportunity to use the new system or tool. Keeping at it when you know it does work and will help is essential (keeping at it with a fundamentally flawed system is less helpful). Making it easier to adopt the change rather than continuing on the old path will also be invaluable.

Implementing change is a deep skill, and project management expertise will be crucial. You don't have to do this all yourself; your broader organisation will contain a lot of knowledge that you may be able to draw on while you act as a sponsor.

Making knowledge explicit

At the heart of what you are doing in the Repeatable stage is moving your contracting process from individual opinions applied in an ad-hoc way to a shared, explicit method. You will need to document your approach for it to be used consistently and, most importantly, improved. Examples of explicit knowledge are templates, playbooks, training materials, checklists, and process maps.

As you do this, consider the following:

- **Making knowledge explicit can be threatening**: If people in your team feel that their value depends on the knowledge in their head, they will be reluctant to share. Early in the exercise, make sure that your team understands the importance—for both the organisation and for them personally—of moving to a more systematised approach, including the opportunity for more exciting work.

- **There is a trade-off between action and control**: The more controls you put in place around who can make changes to your playbooks and templates, the slower you'll move and the less participation you'll get in suggesting modifications. It's all too easy to kill continuous improvement in practice, so I urge you to take a liberal approach and allow team members to make changes. The reality is that it's better to get less-than-perfect contractual approaches documented, explicit and capable of being improved than for sub-optimal hidden practices to continue.

- **Avoid creating too many documents**: Documents are excellent places to hide knowledge. They act like coffins (and document management systems act like graveyards). Try to keep this explicit knowledge in as few places as possible and err on the side of storing it in wiki pages (i.e., your own private Wikipedia) rather than documents.

- **Consistency across regions**: Multi-national organisations will have challenges with adopting a consistent approach, so start with the larger centres and see if you can find ways to highlight local exceptions rather than accept completely different methods.

- **Gravitate towards more structure**: There is a continuum of how structured your knowledge is, with entirely free-form documents at one end and databases at the other. Different types of knowledge can sit in various places along that spectrum. However, try to move towards more structure. If in doubt, try to use a table rather than an essay to document positions and hold clauses in databases rather than in old contracts sitting on a shelf in your office.

- **It's not about the technology**: We spend a lot of time refining Radiant Law's systems, but that doesn't mean that technology is the priority. What matters most is building a culture of shared learning.

- **Support common standards**: There aren't many standards in contracting beyond the standard terms that have emerged in the financial, property, and construction industries, but try to encourage their emergence where you can, as we could all do with a simpler life.

Finally, making knowledge explicit is about individuals. The reality (which conflicts with what we would like it to be) is that a few people will make a vast contribution and that single-handed Herculean efforts are what makes the difference between a helpful system and one that's ignored. Though we encourage everyone to participate, it's the few who will make all the difference, and it's worth rewarding their efforts.

Who is going to perform contracting?

For some years, we've been watching a new pattern emerge in the more forward-thinking enterprises for supporting the legal aspects of their contracting.

This approach draws on the outsourcing fundamental that companies should develop expertise in core areas while outsourcing non-core activities that specialists can better provide. We documented this as a model identifying who should do what:

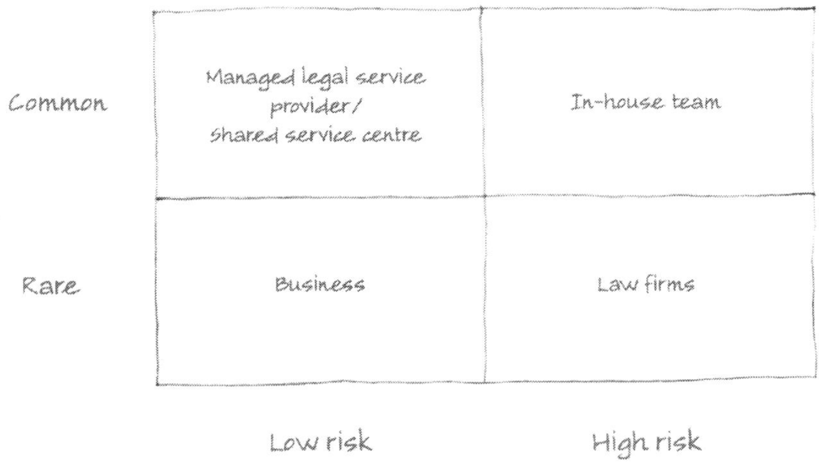

Figure 5 - Support model for contracting

This approach has four different groups supporting the contracts:

- **In-house teams**: If you have lots of similar high-value contracts, getting good at delivering them may make sense as a core activity for your business. The large technology providers, for example, tend to have teams of specialised negotiators.

- **Law firms**: For relatively rare, specialised, and high-risk contracts, it makes sense to rely on expert advisors at law firms rather than hire employees. The question then becomes how to buy these services smartly (especially given how expensive law firms have become). You can scope the project, give clear instructions, fix fees, disaggregate the work, and push parts to alternative service providers, and you can build long-term relationships with law firms to create more value.

- **Business**: Moving to the bottom-left quadrant, it's reasonable to expect the business to safely support the low-risk, low-complexity but high-variability work that doesn't particularly matter. The question in this context is: how do you help the business to help itself? This is where training, policies, standard terms, and self-help tools come in.

- **Managed legal service providers/shared service centre**: When you have high volumes of simple and medium-complexity contracts (the top-left of the matrix), the business can reasonably look to legal and ask for a solution. Larger organisations may elect to build a specialised team in an (often offshore) shared service centre or turn to a third-party managed legal services provider (Radiant Law's specialism).

This model tends to change over time as your contracting approach becomes more sophisticated:

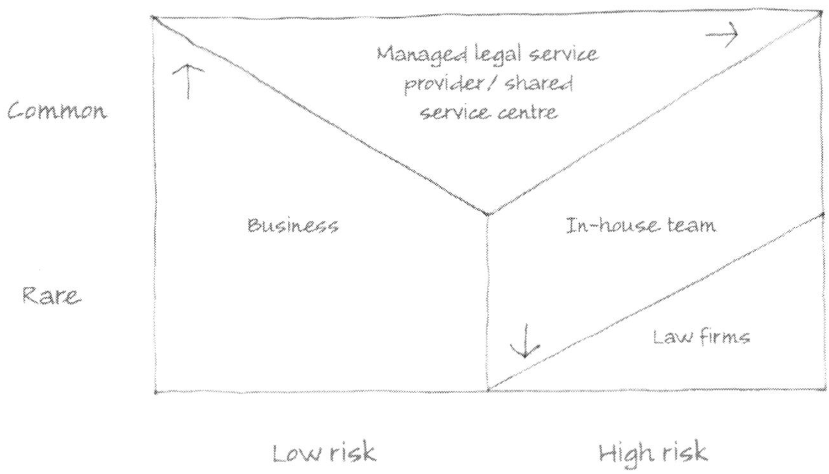

Figure 6 - Advanced support model for contracting

A few things are going on in the picture above:

- We have extended the role of the business. In the same spirit as doing your own shopping checkout, we want to increase self-service in the business by giving it the tools to safely handle more by itself.

- The shared service centre or managed legal services provider should, over time, be taking on more complex work as part of "taming" additional types of contracts.

- In turn, the in-house team should be upskilling to become capable of handling more of the work that would otherwise be sent to law firms. This instantly delivers additional cost savings and makes their roles more engaging.

- The law firms' role reduces over time. While there will always be a need for specialist advice on the hardest of deals, most law firms are too busy pricing themselves out of the market to be used more generally.

The overall impact of this evolution is a significant reduction in the total cost of support, with a greater emphasis on technology, self-service, and codified knowledge, in addition to an upskilled in-house team focused on more stimulating work.

The trick, of course, is not to see this as just a way to move the cost from one budget (legal) to another (business). Your goal is to reduce the activities required on the more straightforward contracts. Expensive senior resources can transfer some of their responsibilities to more empowered juniors, allowing them to work on the more complex transactions and challenges the business faces[42].

---

[42] Pushing work down to the lowest competent level is a core concept in Lean, but it is often resisted in the legal world. The need for "judgement" is the biggest blocker, but with tools such as playbooks and the availability of senior lawyers to give their view on more nuanced points, junior team members can do a lot more.

These changes won't just affect who is working on which contracts; they'll also increase the demand for additional skills, which we have already seen with the rise of legal operations roles. These roles are significant because there is now somewhere to delegate improvement activities[43]. The result is that more progressive GCs with larger teams will have a new way to unlock improvements.

We are also seeing a shift in who is seen as the expert. Traditionally, expertise in contracting has resided with law firms. Partners held forth on what matters while their clients struggled to evaluate who knew best[44], and their incentives led to complexity everywhere. Several things have now changed:

- a few leading companies have demonstrated that contracting can be far slicker in practice without suffering the disasters meant to befall those who don't adopt complexity-over-everything,

- there is a gathering movement on the edges of the legal industry of thinkers that are pushing for a more enlightened approach to contracting, which the RADICAL approach builds upon, and

- there are new types of providers, like Radiant Law, who have changed the incentives and brought together broader skills to support their clients.

---

[43] We have found that the most effective way of making changes is for the whole team to treat continuous improvement as a key part of their role, but if that's not possible, relying on legal ops is a pragmatic fallback. Legal ops roles can also introduce skills into the mix that may be missing.

[44] Economists call this an information asymmetry problem and describe legal services as an example of "credence goods", i.e., goods whose qualities can't be observed by the customer after purchase.

We are starting to see clients move beyond just buying traditional brands. They are now relying more on metrics and results. Contracting is becoming more tangible, and it's getting easier to identify high quality through numbers[45].

Whose paper?

There's a massive advantage in your paper[46] being the starting point of a negotiation:

- there are only so many points that the other side can raise in practice, and it gives you a boost out of the gate on smaller topics[47],
- it significantly reduces the effort involved in the negotiation stage (you know your way around your template, and
- you can set the tone for the subsequent negotiations.

Given that there is so much value in using your paper, prioritise producing strong templates to use in common deals. You're creating far more work for yourself if you must keep using the other side's drafts rather than creating your own template. However, unless it's completely relevant, insisting on your paper for a specialist deal is unhelpful. You may have all the negotiating leverage in the world,

[45] For example, you can ask for data on response and turnaround times and net promoter scores to understand how well different suppliers perform.

[46] "Your paper" means that the first draft of the contract was created by you—hopefully using a template.

[47] "Reasonable" terms cover a range of possible outcomes. If a provision is good enough for the other side, they will usually accept the clause even if it's not optimal. This creates an opportunity to fine tune your terms, avoiding lengthy negotiations while obtaining good outcomes.

but a software licence is not going to be remotely appropriate for a software-as-a-service deal. Your ability to always use your templates will also vary depending on leverage and conventions. Still, it's a lot easier to persuade the other side to use your paper if it's short, clear, reasonable, and relevant, which we'll explore further in the next chapter.

The consequences of working from the other side's paper are:

- You'll use a more general and principle-led playbook, but that will probably only exist if you do a lot of those deals, and if you do, are you sure you can't move them to your paper?

- You may well go straight to a "red flag" risk analysis and then to signature if you have only a low degree of negotiation leverage for the deal.

- This is one of the two scenarios where artificial intelligence[48] plays a role in contracting (spotting issues in the other side's paper), but as I'll explain later, and like the playbook issue, in practice, you probably won't have an AI system carefully calibrated to your organisational risk tolerance for transactions that only happen occasionally.

Summary

This chapter looked at some of the fundamental underpinning principles that will apply in the Repeatable stage and beyond. I set out a generic structure for thinking about your contracting:

[48] Artificial intelligence or AI in contracting usually means machine learning and natural language processing—technologies that can be used to try to identify key data points and recognise particular types of clauses. Bear in mind that the grand term of "artificial intelligence" has very little to do with actual intelligence.

initiation, drafting, negotiation, signing, and management. I covered how to implement change, with a strong emphasis on quick projects rather than transformational change. I talked about the importance of making knowledge explicit so your team have a standard and thus improvable way of working. I examined how to resource your contracting processes and the value in building a support ecosystem that includes both internal and external providers. Finally, I discussed the implications of whether or not you use your templates.

Now that we've covered the basics, let's look at the problems in the Repeatable stage and the solutions you can apply. Getting these fundamentals in place will put your contracting process on the right footing to start using technology.

Chapter 4 Repeatable: The Steps

It's now time to learn how to implement the Repeatable stage principles. Here are the tools and processes to put in place in the Repeatable stage (I've added a "Track" column for managing your contracting process).

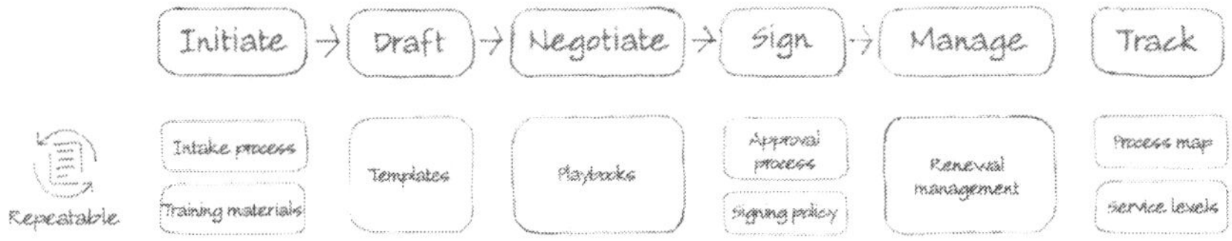

Figure 7 - Repeatable stage steps

These are the core building blocks for a successful process, but don't worry about perfection at this point. You just want to get something in place that can be used and then improved.

Intake and service levels

The problem

How best to enable business users to request help with their contracts?

The solution

- Create a form for starting the process so that the necessary information can be collected the first time, improving consistency and avoiding going back and forth. Consider giving the business team the ability to create simple contracts themselves.

- Create a process that enables requests to be sent to a single place so that the contracting team can triage them and decide who should support them. There may be different places to go in large organisations for particular contracts (e.g., procurement v sales).

- Define target service levels for acknowledging and completing responses, so the initiator has some predictability and can plan accordingly.

- The contracting team could set minimum thresholds to avoid needing to be involved in low-risk contracts (covered in the next section).

Points to consider

At some point, someone in the business is going to need assistance with a contract. They will need somewhere to send their request and will undoubtedly appreciate a prompt response in a predictable timeframe.

Too often, this critical stage is ill-defined. The initiator asks the person who helped them last time, there's some to-ing and fro-ing with questions, and finally, something happens. This approach, while common, is neither good for the contracts team nor the business. Contract team members may like to be liked, but high performance is rewarded with too many requests and over-work. It's not sustainable. An unstructured approach also means that time and effort is spent gathering the needed information—it's slow and inefficient for everyone involved.

The better approach is a formal intake process with a central place to ask for help and a structured form to collect relevant information. No one likes completing forms but gathering this information avoids going back and forth every time; the questions, of course, should be kept to an absolute minimum[49].

[49] You may encounter "evaders"—individuals who try to avoid the process, only

Not being able to go to their favourite helper also won't appeal to the business. Still, clear service levels for responding and completing the activity are the quid pro quo for the intake process change. In the Refinement stage, you're going to measure and improve the actual performance against the service levels, but don't let that stop you from now starting to keep track.

Identifying risks

Problem

How can you make sure that risks in your contracts are being checked and approved by the right people?

Solution

We will be covering a more comprehensive approach to contract risk management in Chapter 8. For now, put in place:

- a risk-based triage as part of the intake process to confirm who is best placed to handle the agreement (which may be the business),
- an approval process so that relevant departments and managers sign off on their part of the agreement and any identified material risks, and
- a signing policy to make sure that an appropriate person signs the contract. The management level required should depend on the risks involved.

---

complete parts of the form, or otherwise don't play nice. How you respond will depend on the culture of your company, but it's better to handle this head on. For example, you might enforce field completion on the form, require additional training for repeat offenders, or provide data back to managers on performance.

Points to consider

Not all contracts are created equal. Some require proper vetting and attention, while others only need the basics checked. Send agreements to the appropriate support, approvers, and signer with a thoughtful process.

Fears about risk have led to the overuse of legal resources, with contracting teams becoming bogged down in reviewing contracts that are probably never going to be significant causes of trouble. You inevitably have limited resources and want to direct them appropriately, so head off low-risk contracts at the initiation stage and free up the contracting team to work on more critical agreements.

The following are typical indicators of whether particular attention is required:

- the value and committed term of the transaction,
- if the contract uses an unmodified standard form,
- if it is just renewing an existing approved deal,
- any material security or reputational risks,
- any granting of guarantees or security,
- any processing of personal data, and
- any material IP being created or transferred.

Some teams specify cut-off rules when they don't need to be involved, such as "less than £X in value, unless they touch on risk areas A, B or C". Others use a points system to determine how risky a contract is. Either way, a stratification of risk is a helpful way to triage work.

Business self-help

Problem

The contracting team doesn't have enough time to support every contract. How can more of the contract drafting process be devolved to the business to help themselves?

Solution

Part of the solution will come at the Robots stage, but there are basics that you can put in place now to help the business do more:

- content that explains unintuitive points to the other side early in the process to head off misunderstandings,
- a playbook and training materials on the issues that you want the business team to cover early on in discussions with the other side,
- user-friendly and straightforward template agreements for use by the business team (these will be automated in the Robots stage), and
- a training programme to make sure that the basics are well understood by the business team.

You should also establish one place for the business team to access these resources, and we'll cover that in the Robots stage.

Points to consider

Getting the business team to the point where they can support themselves with more straightforward contracts and do more work in the early stages of more complex transactions is attractive. Still, you need to take the following into account:

- it needs to be done safely,
- everyone has plenty to do already, so if you're just passing work to the next-door department, it will take them as long as it does you and won't be helping the organisation, and
- you need to simplify tasks you're giving to people with less training.

Standard templates

Problem

How do you get more deals onto your paper and reduce the amount of time spent on multiple rounds of negotiations?

Solution

Create a suite of modular standard templates for the most common deal types that are short, clear, reasonable, and relevant.

Points to consider

As noted in the previous chapter, using your templates at the start of the deal offers many advantages. That will be more likely if your templates not only exist but are also fit for purpose and easy to digest by the other side. I argued that terms should be more reasonable, going straight to the middle ground. Your goal should also be short, clear, and relevant terms.

The **length**, it turns out, is particularly relevant. It has a dramatic effect on first impressions, and an agreement of only a few pages is far more likely to be looked at quickly and accepted.

Case Study: Shorter Terms

As an example of shortening terms, we took one client's contract and reduced it from about fourteen pages to three.
We didn't lose any of the material points in the agreement through this reduction, which illustrates how unnecessarily verbose typical legal language is.

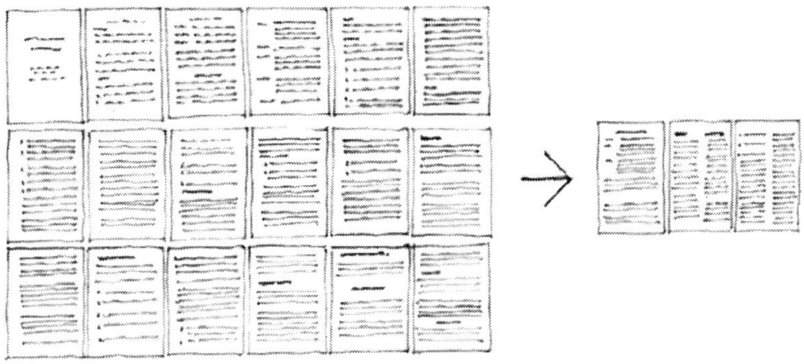

Figure 8 - Simplifying a Contract

As part of this exercise, we also changed a few unreasonable provisions to some that were more mainstream but still addressed the client's real concerns. We moved the agreement's specifics up front, making the commercial details the focus of the document.

The result was we reduced the average time to signature from months to just days, with fewer than 10 per cent of the agreements requiring negotiation. The reasonableness of the terms, not just the length, was also critical to the result.

Case Study 4 - Shorter Terms

As you shorten and simplify your agreements (if no one can remember why a provision was included, this might be an excellent time to get rid of it), you'll also want to **clarify** the language.

The drive towards clear contracts is part of the Plain English movement, but clear contracts are still contracts. The language of contracting is inevitably somewhat technical because we want contracts to be rigorous and enforceable, as well as usable. There is less tolerance for ambiguity and inconsistency of terminology than is acceptable with other written works.

Halfway between code and prose, contracts need special rules, and I commend to you *A Manual of Style for Contract Drafting* by Ken Adams as the go-to text on how to phrase your contracts. As a keen advocate of removing words, using thought-through terminology, and careful handling of potential ambiguities, Ken brings to contracts a rigour that is much needed to challenge the passed-down habits that have characterised much thinking in this area to date. Ken's work also lifts the lid on how awful most contract drafting is.

In addition to clarifying the language, look at how you structure your contract. Try to design it to make it more accessible and more acceptable to the other side. Consider the order and structure (key terms up front, legal issues afterwards, and the particularly dull topics right at the back) and make it data-oriented (separating the data points or otherwise making them easy to extract[50]).

Finally, your terms need to be **relevant** and focused on the essential provisions for the deal. They should not include "just in case" provisions (helping with length, too). Make your terms modular

[50] See, for example, content controls in Word https://docs.microsoft.com/en-us/office/vba/word/concepts/working-with-word/working-with-content-controls

and maintain a separate library (which can be a shared document in the first iteration) of clauses relevant in less common circumstances. This will be a lot easier to manage once you've implemented the document automation described in the Robots section.

There will be a trade-off between relevance and the frequency with which you handle a deal of a particular type. It's not worth having templates for the less common agreements, and trying to impose overly generic terms will often slow a deal down rather than speed it up. There are times when accepting the use of the other side's terms with dignity is a virtue.

Despite this, err on the side of having your own good templates:

- Producing an initial draft from a contract template is significantly faster than working from old deals.

- Good templates help ensure that your team considers the relevant issues, lead to better drafting, and make the final contract more consistent and predictable (greatly enhancing your ability to manage the contract).

- Templates are the foundation for further development, forming the basis for several additional stages of improving your contracting processes, including document automation and playbooks.

- With a consistent set of agreements, it is easier to update them as laws change, review them to identify variations in positions taken, or extract key data points.

Generally, templates have a leveraging effect. If they're good, you'll see the impact across your contracting process—likewise, if they're bad. Consistency through standard terms is better than inconsistency (unless you consistently send out agreements with the same error in them). The upshot is that time invested in improving your contract templates more than pays for itself. Bake these types of values into your business cases, even if it's just a stab.

Playbooks

Problem

How do you improve the consistency of negotiations and control risk during the negotiation phase?

Solution

Create a playbook for each standard template and any other common agreements that you review on the other side's paper, along with a process for updating them. Appoint one or more owners to approve inclusions and proactively update the playbooks.

Points to consider

By creating standard terms, you effectively crystallise your preferred positions on the different topics that come up within a given type of agreement. What this doesn't help with is:

- when the other side raises issues with your draft, or
- when you're working with the other side's first draft.

Traditionally, the answer is to make it up as you go along, depending on the reviewer involved and what their mood is. This makes the expertise in your team hard to share and the negotiation process even harder to standardise.

The solution is a playbook. It's a document that captures what to do when you see an issue that regularly comes up in a negotiation. There are effectively two types of playbooks:

- **The other side's paper**: When reviewing the other side's paper, the playbook is likely to be a list of points based on principle, often structured as points you want to see covered in the agreement and points that you don't want to appear.

- **Your paper**: When it's your agreement, you should structure the playbook by following the underlying template's order (with a few general points up front). You will find it reasonably easy to predict where the other side will raise issues.

Whoever owns it, the playbook should be a structured repository of knowledge and presented as a table:

Clause	Issue	Action	Reason

Figure 9 - Playbook structure

If you want to create a discursive explanation of topics and points, keep them in separate documents. Playbooks are practical tools, and every word you add slows the user down, so keep them as tight as possible. Don't seek exhaustive completeness; if you keep adding rows, your playbook will eventually become unusable. Instead, focus on the key issues.

To get going, I suggest you get an experienced member of your team to create a simple starting point, or if you're feeling inclusive, get several team members to identify the most common issues and come up with the standard responses. It would help if you then implemented a rule that every time someone asks for advice on a new material point, they should include the answer in the playbook. Your playbook should be a living document, so you need to have a process in place to ensure it is updated regularly and everyone is using the latest version.

Another challenge you may experience is that it's a lot easier, emotionally, to treat every decision as unique and avoid committing to a standard position. We often see teams being reluctant to decide on an authoritative answer to a particular situation—and then they're surprised that they can't get these contracts off their desks. If a change is exceptional, at least try to define when the exception applies. The rules could refer to, for example, the size of the deal and its strategic importance. There will always be situations where escalations are needed, and you can specify these in the playbook.

One thing to consider is whether you can give playbooks to the business users to help move the early stages of negotiations "upstream". With this use case, you need to keep it extremely simple with clear "if-then" rules and triggers for when to refer to legal. Including more in-depth explanations can be tempting, but try to keep it to the point.

Finally, it's often better to get rid of a negotiation point than to capture it in a playbook. When issues come up, consider if you can get rid of them by tweaking your standard terms. Similarly, rather than having multiple fallback steps in your playbook, perhaps you could go straight to the end position to speed up discussions?

Process maps

Problem

How do you turn a stream of emails and documents into a shared understanding of the process?

Solution

Map your processes, share them with the team, and use them as the cornerstone of your future Robot and Refinement stage activities.

Points to consider

The realities of your current contracting processes are probably even more complex, convoluted, and inconsistent than you fear, but that's fixable. The starting point is to understand "as-is" reality, and there's nothing like a picture to make things clear.

Our preferred starting visualisation is a swim lane diagram—a flowchart overlaid onto "swim lanes" representing the different participants. Here's a simplified example:

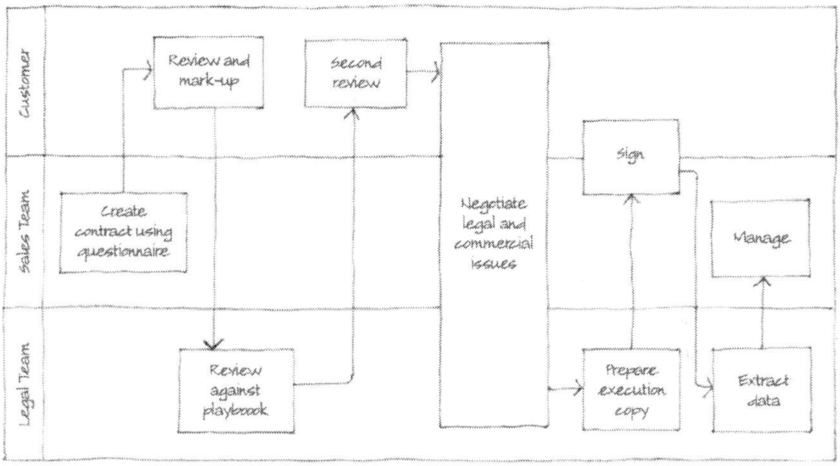

Figure 10 - Swimlane diagram

The easiest way to create one is with a few people who are intimately familiar with the process, a whiteboard, Post-it notes for the steps, and pens for the arrows. Don't worry at the beginning about what the process should look like. Just focus on what happens—the "as-is". Use different-coloured Post-it notes to represent the value the step delivers in meeting the stakeholders' needs:

- steps that are adding real value,
- steps that are not adding real value but are necessary (at least for now), and
- steps that are not adding value.

Now is also an excellent time to start counting. I talk about data in detail in Chapter 7, but for now, begin to collect data on:

- how many deals you are doing,
- the average time spent working on the deal in each stage,
- the average time a deal stays in each stage, and
- the most common obstacles faced by your team.

The answers will give you an excellent view of the waste and delays in the process[51].

Once you understand what is happening (in as much detail as possible), you can think about the "to-be". You're pretty much guaranteed to get some quick wins from this process, as once you

---

[51] You can start to compare, for example, the time that is spent actually doing the work (called the process time) against the time in the stage (the lead time). For a review of a document, it will probably be an hour or two of process time and days or weeks of lead time. Not a great ratio, but common for services at an early stage of development.

If you are interested in exploring this area more, see Karen Martin and Mike Osterling's book *Value Stream Mapping*.

understand what's going on, you'll spot steps that just don't make sense, are not adding value, and are not necessary. You'll want to keep refining, removing steps where possible, and ensuring that you focus as much effort as possible on the things that add the most value.

We will come back to improvements in the Refinement stage, but for now, enjoy getting a glimpse into the underlying madness of your organisation.

Summary

In this chapter, I've covered the basics you need to put in place for your contracting process:

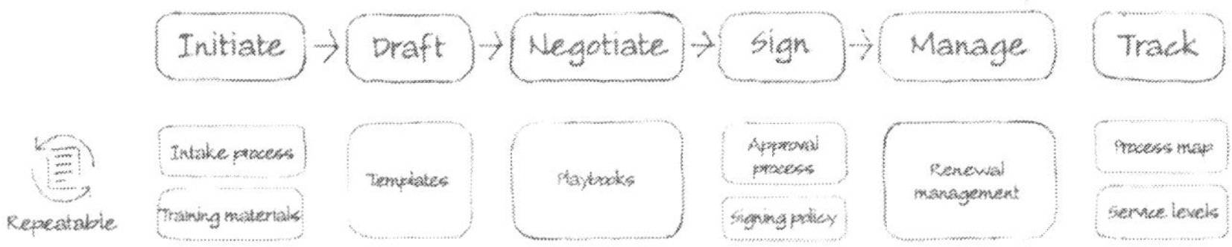

None of the parts will be great at first, and that's OK. Greatness comes from iteratively improving them over time, and there will always be things to improve. Most importantly, once you've completed these steps, you will be ready for automation, which is much more fun. Onwards!

Chapter 5 Robots: Core Principles

Now that you've got the basics in place, let's look at applying technology. At this point, I would gently remind you that there are no silver bullets, and you're not going to solve everything with a shiny new system, no matter how breathlessly the salesperson describes its features. With that in mind, I will start with an overview of the different types of available systems and what they do, explain why AI will not save you, and highlight the value of using what you already have. In the next chapter, I will detail which systems to focus on and how to get the most from them.

Using technology to help with contracting dates back to at least the 1970s, but there has been a recent explosion in the options available for automating your contracting process. Depending on your predilections, you'll either consider the range of options to be deeply daunting or like a sweet shop to your inner child.

The truth is that not all that glitters is gold. Putting a system in place doesn't necessarily mean it will have a significant impact, either because it will turn out only to fix a small part of the overall problem (which is common) or it will not get used (which is even more common).

What technology is available?

There isn't a general recognised category of "ContractTech", but beyond just email and Word, there is technology for sales, procurement, and legal teams related to contracts.

To try to make sense of the very noisy technology world, here's a map of how the different specialised products fit into the stages of the contracting process:

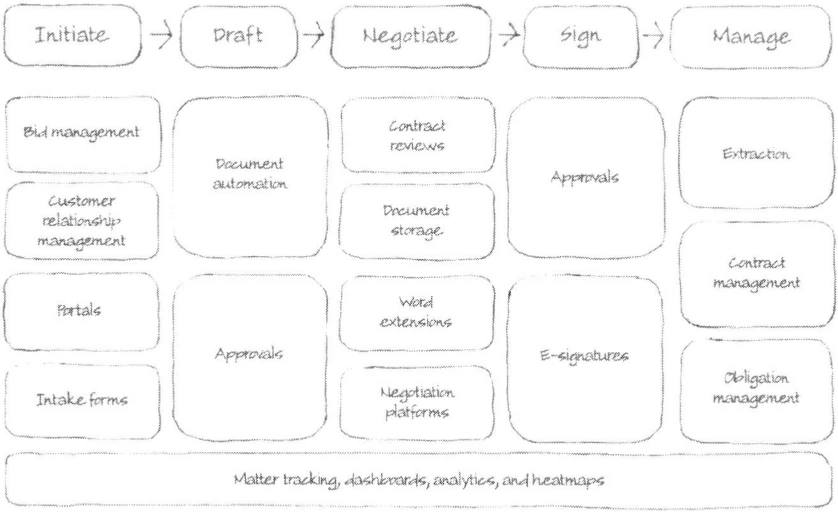

Figure 11 - Types of contract technology

Here's what they do:

Initiate

- **Bid management**: A general term for a range of procurement systems covering requests for proposals, auctions, and other bid processes.

- **Customer relationship management**: A system used by the sales team for tracking leads and opportunities. Opportunities may eventually become contracts, so this can be a feeder system for the contracting process and even the record system for the outcome.

- **Portal**: A single place on your intranet for the business (and contracting) team to go to for self-service resources and help.

- **Intake forms**: Forms for the business to complete to get help from the contracting team, ensuring that the relevant information is gathered and potentially starting a matter-tracking process.

Draft

- **Document automation**: Systems that let the contracting team (or the business) generate tailored contracts based on answers to questions.

- **Drafting approvals**: Systems to automate the approvals process for drafted contracts (such as those created by the business) or approve the business's instructions.

Negotiate

- **Contract reviews**: AI tools to flag issues in contracts on the other side's paper that are based on whether particular types of clauses appear (or not).

- **Document storage**: Online places to store draft agreements (and potentially emails) so that other team members can access them.

- **Word extensions**: Additional buttons for Word to help lawyers format, check and update contracts during negotiations, as well as access clause databases.

- **Negotiation platforms**: Online negotiation tools that allow participants to amend contracts in the browser rather than send documents back and forth by email.

Sign

- Signing approvals: For collecting approvals before signature on finalised contracts.

- E-signatures: Systems for signing documents online, avoiding the need for printing and wet-ink signatures.

Manage

- **Extraction**: AI tools for extracting key data points from signed contracts or reviewing a collection of signed contracts to find provisions[52].

- **Contract management**: Systems for storing signed contracts and associated data.

- **Obligation management**: Systems for tracking the performance of obligations under contracts.

Track

- **Matter tracking and dashboards**: Systems for tracking the status of all your deals, usually with a dashboard showing performance against key measures.

- **Heatmaps**: Data analytics tools to display which parts of your contracts are negotiated most.

Point v end-to-end solutions

Not all the tools described above are necessarily distinct. You can buy a system that gives you many different capabilities. Whether you should do this is a trade-off between two competing approaches by the suppliers, who offer either:

---

[52] This can be particularly helpful when doing due diligence for mergers and acquisitions.

- **Point solutions**: systems that just do one thing and not much else and are often very good at what they do.

- **End-to-end solutions**: systems that support the contracting process from initiation through to contract management[53]. They may not be as good at any particular activity as a point solution, but they have the advantage of connecting all the parts.

Choosing between the approaches can be difficult. A good point solution will probably be better at the one thing it does, but an end-to-end solution may be good enough. Point solutions can often be integrated with other systems, but they can be a pain. End-to-end solutions come with integration (at least between the different contracting stages) but are less flexible, often opinionated, and may not be ideal for all your use cases. Then, there are the end-to-end solutions that tick every box in the contracting process but are weak at every stage (some of the older contract management systems, I'm looking at you).

We prefer point solutions at Radiant Law, but we've had to learn how to build the integrations needed to make things work together. There's no correct answer to this other than not being paralysed by indecision. If in doubt, go with the simplest possible solution to meet your needs.

One final point: your organisation is bigger than the contracting process. Consider whether there are other systems spanning your organisation. The contracting module of an ERP[54] system may not

---

[53] Often, these suppliers came out of the contract management world and expanded to earlier stages of the contracting process to cover the full contract lifecycle.

[54] Enterprise resource planning—a unified (but, in practice, often clumsy) system

be best in class, but there may be good reasons to use it rather than introduce another (unintegrated) system. The more "end-to-end" your proposed system is, the more likely it is to run up against other systems in your organisation, raising integration and usage challenges.

Case Study: The Upgrade

A company sold complex products, not helped by the sales team regularly going off-piste and creating new variations. The finance team struggled to track the deals, and millions of pounds were lost each year due to poor invoicing. The company introduced a new intake system that was integrated with the contract management system and used a complex form that had to be completed by the sales team.

The company collected better data, but there were issues: the system's champion left the company and wasn't replaced. The integration between the systems turned out to be brittle, meaning that updates to the intake form often required changes by multiple teams of programmers (who had other priorities). The form collected more data than necessary, making it unpopular with the sales team. The project was also underfunded.

Eighteen months later, the contracting process was still slower than before the system had been introduced.

Case Study 5 - The Upgrade

Databases, workflows, and document transformation

It's easy to be overwhelmed by all the technology available, but the systems are generally pretty straightforward and usually combine one or more of three core technologies:

---

for running a company's business processes.

- **Databases**: a structured way of saving data,
- **Workflow**: a way to manage the flow of tasks between different people (and automate parts of the journey), and
- **Document transformation**: a way of creating documents and converting them to different formats.

Not exactly rocket science.

This breakdown gives us some more insight into the point v end-to-end solution debate. In an ideal world, you wouldn't want to keep your data in more than one database, and you would like to store as much data as possible. Right now, we're usually throwing away most of the data associated with contracting (or at least it's inaccessible), and we're generally not using the data that is to hand. Even in the most sophisticated of end-to-end systems, the level of data analytics is pretty crude. The market leaders use separate analytical tools, but you can see that end-to-end systems—or at least a unified data store—will have an advantage in the long term.

Similarly, with workflow, there is value in modelling and controlling the flow of the end-to-end contracting process. Taken to its logical conclusion, this means bringing all the participants in the negotiation together on a negotiation platform, thus removing the need for email and Word. It's a great idea, but it has a serious problem. In every negotiation, the other party will have to adopt the system instead of continuing with their usual way of working. Anyone who has tried to roll out a system with their team will understand how challenging this is. Some suppliers are working on making their negotiation platform as simple as possible, and perhaps one day this will get traction, but not yet.

Even if you scale back your ambitions and just try to model your internal processes, there can be real challenges. Expect the refinement to take far longer than you bargained for, as reality turns out to be highly complicated and the path of emails convoluted. Be careful, therefore, about how much you bite off at first, and bear in mind that a bit of flexibility, such as using email for some parts of the process, may be better than trying to move everything into one system.

Finally, the document transformation elements (e.g., document automation and e-signatures) underline how document-centric the contracting process is, despite automation. Even if companies can find their signed contracts, they are often scanned PDFs that require optical character recognition[55] and AI to extract data points at scale.

This brings us to the thorny topic of AI.

Artificial intelligence

If ever there were an example of a silver bullet wannabe, it's AI. The potential of machine learning and natural language processing has been greeted with much excitement by customers who hope it will fix all their problems. And plenty of legal tech suppliers are keen to sell them anything. The only problem with this union of demand and supply is that it turns out that AI can't do that much for contracts.

While AI can translate contractual language into another language, break down the parts of the sentence, spot dates and amounts, and—most usefully for our purposes—classify a clause as a particular type[56], the system cannot tell you what the clause means[57]. We aren't even close on this one.

---

[55] Optical character recognition or OCR is an often-wrong way of turning a scan into searchable text.

Turning back to the chart, it's perhaps unsurprising, therefore, that there are only a couple of types of systems that use AI:

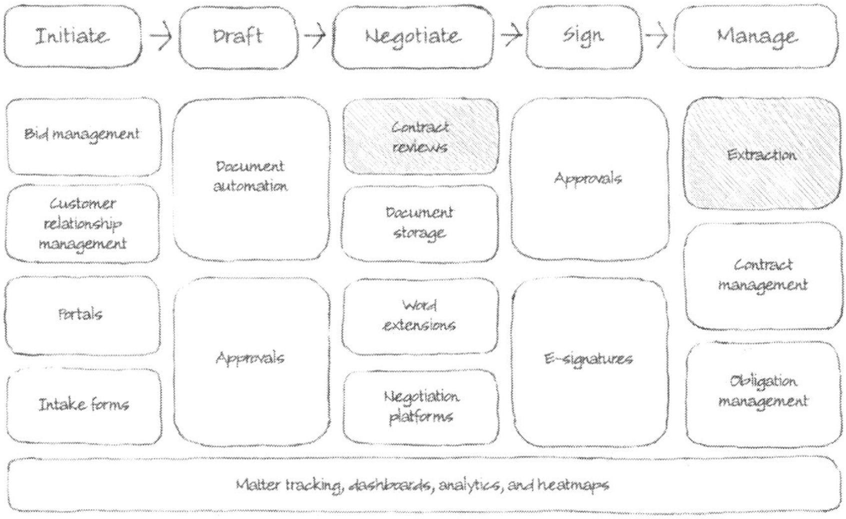

Figure 12 - Where AI fits in

Contract review: These are tools to review the other side's paper to spot issues. These tools are clever. They let you build rules for whether you want to see or not see clauses of a particular type and then warn you about what they find. The results are a bit crude, both because they aren't 100 per cent reliable at finding clauses of a particular type and because the system doesn't know what the clause means. You're still going to need to read and mark up the agreement and then negotiate it to fix any problems found.

---

[56] Accuracy is about seventy-something per cent in the wild, sometimes up to 90 per cent plus depending on how distinctive the clause is.

[57] Finding the termination of change of control clauses is admittedly helpful when buying companies, but more often we need to interpret clauses, not just find them, which still requires humans.

These tools can speed up the review process and provide another pair of eyes, which improves consistency if you get a lot of contracts of a particular type. But this raises another question: why are you receiving so many agreements on the other side's paper? The best solution would be to use your paper instead[58].

Extraction: This covers tools with two use cases. The first is extracting data as part of getting contracts into a contract management system. The second is for document reviews as part of major one-off events (legislative changes, acquisitions, etc.). These tools help, but before we consider it revolutionary, let's be clear about what's going on: you are replacing paralegals with a faster and cheaper tool. What you do with the data is more important than how you review the contracts.

So, there isn't that much that AI can currently offer contracting, and it certainly won't solve the "contracting problem".

Some final thoughts:

- When developing your standard terms, it helps to run them through one or more contract review systems to ensure that you aren't throwing up unnecessary automated objections.

- The extraction tools underline the value of holding a data representation of a contract. Suppose you are using document automation to create the first draft of an agreement. Even if some parts of the contract change during negotiations, you have most of the information you need

[58] There is another problem associated with the system ideally needing to be configured for your organisation's particular concerns and risk appetite (rather than relying on the system defaults), which is it's only justified when using it multiple times for the same type of agreement. Again, better to use your own terms.

about its content in a structured form, so don't throw it away.

- Most of the AI tools out there are a pretty interface on open-source (as in free) AI libraries that are getting better all the time. We're going to see increasingly powerful systems become available at lower and lower costs. Bear this in mind before making significant financial commitments.

Further considerations

Some other points to consider as you adopt your robots:

- **Fewer tools:** Although users have lots of tools available, they only use a handful in practice. The usage tails off fast after the first two or three they use daily. If a user isn't using an application daily, they will tend to forget about it. If you think about what lawyers use, the first two positions are inevitably taken by email and Word. If you are hoping your users will adopt a new system, think about what else it will be competing with and whether other tools need to be dropped rather than just accumulating more.

- **Flexibility v completeness:** It's tempting with a new system to seek completeness—making sure that it does everything. Be aware, though, that your use cases will change, and in practice, what you think are vital priorities may go unused (we're regularly wrong on this front). We've found that giving users flexible and general tools is usually more helpful in the long run than a specific system[59].

---

[59] It's no accident that Microsoft has done as well as it has with the Office suite, and Office 365 offers powerful automation systems.

- **Start with what you have:** Your IT department probably doesn't care as much about your problems as you might wish. They have a lot on their hands, and the contracting process generally isn't their top priority. Instead, they're trying to use fewer systems, introduce better integrations, improve security, and get business users actually using the systems they begged for. So before reaching for a shiny new system, consider using what already exists in your environment. You probably have a central place to store things (SharePoint or Google Sites), a ticketing system for intake, data analytics tools, etc. Using what you have is your best starting option, unless you're ready to sign up to a cloud service with a credit card, can take advantage of another department's project, or can create an overwhelming business case for your project.

- **Get going with something:** We regularly see companies caught up in complex evaluations of the many systems available in the market. The larger the company is, the worse this process can be. Implementing pretty much anything is better than analysis paralysis. Don't let your ambitions get ahead of practicalities. A late and expensive project that cannot deliver on what it promised is a poor way to win hearts and minds. Better to crack on with something simple and build on it over time.

- **Open source:** Open source is one of the most potent technology developments of our time, yet it has a poor reputation in some quarters. There has been a Cambrian explosion of software libraries and systems, often better than the commercial alternatives. Legal tech has been mainly proprietary to date, and any open systems or standards have been the exception rather than the rule. However, we're now starting to see significant systems emerge that are not only extremely powerful but also free. If you're having problems getting IT's attention, try asking them to install an open-source system for you. The most important of these for our purposes at the time of writing is Docassemble, a document automation system. You can find other examples for workflow, and open source dominates in AI.

- **A word about Word:** Finally, we should talk about Word. It's the primary tool for contracts and it's used by almost every lawyer[60], but it's also the most abused technology. I shudder to think how much time has been wasted by lawyers fiddling around with formatting documents. To give you a sense of the time lost, we've built extensions for Word, adding features that save lawyers from having to make manual changes, and it now takes us about half the time to mark up a contract as it did previously. Your team can also save vast amounts of time by just learning to use Word properly and there are many excellent training courses on the internet. If your team isn't using standard styles templates across documents, keyboard shortcuts, automated cross-referencing, and track changes, they're doing it wrong.

Summary

This chapter introduced a wide variety of specialist systems and discussed the difference between point v end-to-end solutions. I was

[60] There are also those using Google Docs, and some are even negotiating contracts directly on these documents. This requires the parties to be comfortable showing their changes as they are made, but if you can make it work, it's a great potential improvement on emailing drafts back and forth.

And there are still pockets of Word Perfect users out there. I'm not sure I can help you if you are one of them.

perhaps a little harsh on artificial intelligence, but it won't save us. Most importantly, I recommended starting with what you have already and keeping it simple.

As exciting as technology projects can be, there is a considerable risk of overblown expectations failing to be met by the technology. Implementation is also part of the challenge— you need long-term cultural change to ensure you get value. Starting small and evolving lets you avoid costly mistakes and get going faster. With that in mind, let's explore which systems help.

Chapter 6 Robots: The Steps

You don't need to implement every type of technology, and probably never will. The ones that we recommend at the Robots stage are:

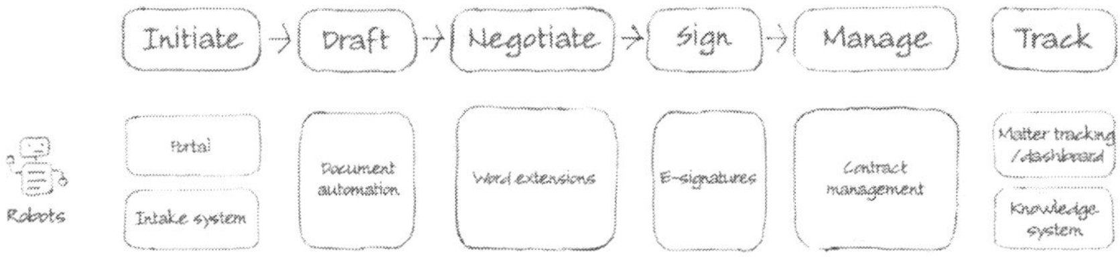

Figure 13 - Robot stage steps

Some of these are specialist contracting tools, but many of them can be covered by repurposing existing platforms within your organisation, at least in the first instance. You will also probably still be using email and Word for the foreseeable future.

I selected these systems because they are the ones that have a real impact. A simple version of each will be good enough for now. It's generally not that hard to migrate to a better system in the future (compared to the effort required in the initial automation), so try to just get going.

Portals and wikis

Problem

How do you get the business team to do more themselves?

Solution

Create a portal as a single launch spot for all assistance related to contracting and keep developing it. Use a wiki as a base knowledge repository (your system will probably come with one).

Points to consider

We are all busy, really busy, and if an activity isn't part of our core job description, it will probably not get much attention. Expecting the broader business team to spend much time on the things you care about is going to be an uphill battle. You're therefore going to need to make it as easy as possible for your business users to find what they need when they need it, and it must be highly usable. Expecting enthusiastic participation in complex training or a lot of information to be retained is a bridge too far. Therefore, make sure that they only need to remember one thing: where to go on the intranet when they need contracting help.

Your company inevitably has an intranet, so you don't need to buy a system. Simply adopt what your company is already using, adding a single unified location for contracting needs. You can link to other systems from there, so you don't need full integration to get the benefits of having a single landing spot. You can build the portal out over time and introduce self-help tools, your intake forms for asking for help, and other training and explanatory materials.

While you're doing this, use the same space for sharing materials within your team. I'm a firm believer in using wikis for this as it allows the team to keep evolving the structure of the information, curate valuable resources, and increase everyone's opportunities to contribute to your knowledge management efforts. Although you may wish to keep the information within the contracting team, err on the side of openness.

In developing your knowledge management system, think about how it will fit into your organisation:

- **Capabilities**: You will want a system for hosting documents that is linked to pages on the wiki (so you can curate your resources). Microsoft SharePoint or Google Sites and Drive can give you all the capabilities you need.

- **The end-to-end contracting process**: Given that the contracting process spans multiple departments, consider how best to work with the other teams to provide relevant information on the end-to-end process.

- **User testing**: However simple, easy, and brilliant your materials are, your users will still misunderstand them. There is no faster way to gain humility than to spend a few minutes watching a business user trying to navigate your creation. I recommend regular user testing.

Your system will need ongoing development. Plenty of legal teams have a page on the intranet, but few have a comprehensive and current resource. Make someone responsible for keeping it up to date and helpful.

I should mention that there has been some excitement about chatbots as a way for end-users to get answers to questions. Whether they help is debatable, but in any case, you would be much better off focusing, at least initially, on providing clear supporting information in more traditional formats.

Intake, matter tracking, and dashboards

Problem

How do you keep track of all the deals you are doing?

Solution

Start to automate your tracking of deals, beginning with the intake process itself and then ongoing deal handling. You can then use the data to understand where the deals are coming from, what they relate to, and how best to deploy your team to support contracts.

Points to consider

Having set up the base intake process in the Repeatable stage, now is the time to add automation.

The intake process can start with something as simple as a single email address (e.g., contractintake@company.com). You can set up mailing lists so that multiple team members can see emails, but make sure there is one person responsible for initial intake to avoid chaos.

Ultimately, you'll want an intake form that gathers comprehensive information. The nature of this information will vary by matter type, but you can create online forms that can ask follow-up questions depending on the answers given to previous ones. As an interim step, you can make interactive PDF or Excel forms that show only questions relevant to the matter. The advantage of these is that they can be emailed to your new intake address, allowing you to get going quickly. Ideally, the intake form will trigger your matter-tracking system once you've implemented it.

Matter-tracking systems allow you to track the status of your deals and capture performance data, too. The status and key metrics can be shown on a dashboard, giving you an overview of workloads and performance. The benefits of these systems include:

- confirming whether you are meetings targets,
- helping balance the load across the team,
- understanding where bottlenecks are occurring, and

- potentially coordinating activities across the broader business.

At its simplest, a matter-tracking system can be a shared spreadsheet (or, even better, a Kanban board[61]) showing who is working on what. You can build something simple in Google Sheets (which, unlike Excel, allows multiple users to edit at the same time) or Trello, Airtable or Coda. Matter tracking helps with the broader challenge of keeping track of external suppliers (including legal spend). Choosing a system often means you must compromise on what you show, but ideally, you want to cover:

- tracking the status of all internal and externally supported deals (with enough data to allow for meaningful analysis of your processes),

- associated financial reporting on fees, and

- workflow to enable hand-offs between departments.

No system covers everything, and few teams have cracked the challenge of coordinating multiple systems. My advice is to accept that you may not have a single view for everything but try to keep to as few systems as possible and prioritise your most pressing needs.

Some systems already within your organisation may be helpful:

---

[61] A Kanban board allows you to move cards (which can represent matters) between columns (representing stages), so you can see the status of each matter. A popular example of Kanban boards is Trello, but many platforms now have this capability.

- **Ticketing systems**: Your IT department is likely to have a ticketing system for tracking IT issues and requests for help. You can repurpose these as a matter-tracking system.

- **Platforms**: You can use SharePoint and Power Automate in Office 365 to create simple workflows that are good enough to get going.

- **Business intelligence tools**: Business analysts in your organisation will probably be using analytics tools that you can repurpose for dashboards.

Document automation

Problem

How can you reduce the time it takes to create contracts from hours or even days to a few minutes while ensuring rigour and consistency?

Solution

Implement a document automation system and start an ongoing process to automate your contracts.

Points to consider

Document automation systems that let you create tailored documents based on the answers to questions are a must-have solution for several reasons:

- **Speed**: Creating a contract using document automation takes a few minutes. You can also create a suite of related documents at the same time, based on the same answers. The business can use document automation to generate simple contracts without needing to talk to legal.

- **Risk management**: Unfortunately, we all regularly make mistakes. Document automation removes many opportunities for error. Document automation also brings rigour to ensure the key issues are addressed in every contract, rather than relying on the user to remember them—it essentially acts as a checklist. It also helps ensure that your users don't use previous deal documents (with provisions negotiated out) for the next agreement.

- **Better contracts**: As issues come up, teams often keep adding points to contracts, and the templates rarely get shortened. There are also limits to how far you can expect a user to tailor a Word version of an agreement for a deal's circumstances. Document automation lets you break out of this cycle. You can tailor your contract each time to only include the relevant issues. The result is shorter documents that are faster to negotiate.

- **Iterative improvements**: Document automation helps you to continuously update your templates (rather than relying on epic redrafting projects). If you know that your users will use the latest version of the template through the system, it's easier to keep making changes to "knock the edges" off your contracts.

- **Happier business**: We've found that the crucial element in determining how business users feel about the contracting process is how quickly they can get going. If you give your business users the ability to create a draft safely using a document automation system, they get a near-instant result—an easy way to be a hero.

There are many document automation systems now on the market. Our favourite is Docassemble, a free and open-source system. If you want a more expensive commercial solution, you have quite a range to choose from: some are powerful and sophisticated, some are pretty and don't do much. As you evaluate the options, consider the following:

- **User interface**: The user interface matters a lot to the users. It needs to be easy to use, ideally to the point where little training is necessary. Beyond that test, beware of weighting eye candy over the other factors on this list.

- **Turning on/off language**: You may already have some simple document automation in your business that can only fill in blanks. These simpler systems don't allow for sections of the document to be turned on and off and cannot handle complex contracts. Make sure that your solution has this feature.

- **Editing**: A simple editing environment will be critical if you want your tech-minded team members to automate templates. Ask for a demo of how this part works and run like hell if it needs serious programmers to create templates. Think through in advance the kinds of customisation your documents are likely to need and ask the vendor to confirm that their system can handle the intricacies[62].

- **Integration**: It's becoming increasingly important to integrate document automation with other systems (through APIs[63]). You may want to get source data from

[62] For a real test, ask the supplier whether their system can handle "repeats within repeats". For example, can the system allow the user to specify an arbitrary number of entities and for each entity specify an arbitrary number of attributes to appear in the contract (such as multiple companies and multiple director details for each of them)?

other systems or send the document straight out through an e-signature system. It's worth checking what integrations exist[64].

- **Browser v Word plugins**: Some contract management system vendors have created Word plugins to provide document automation capabilities. The browser-based systems tend to be much more powerful.

- **Hosting**: All legal tech now comes with a cloud option, and many of the newer ones are only cloud-based. Cloud-based systems will be faster to implement. Ensure you know at the beginning of the selection process whether your IT department will insist on only using systems hosted in their own data centres.

- **Licensing model**: Some suppliers charge a flat fee per organisation, some charge per end-user or document. Check that you aren't going to be accidentally paying a fortune for the system as usage grows.

- **Approvals**: Some of the systems offer additional functionality for adjacent parts of the contracting process, such as approvals. This can be helpful when a business user creates a document, but legal wants to check it before it goes out.

---

[63] API stands for "application programming interface", a way for one system to talk directly to another without needing to involve humans.

[64] If you are going to rely on the API, ask someone technical to review the API documentation. Effective APIs are notoriously hard to find in legal tech.

- **Analytics and reporting**: Some systems are better than others at tracking usage and allowing reporting. These reports can clarify where you have take-up of the system and identify opportunities for improvement.

Remember that choosing a system is the easy part. We will be covering the automation process in the Refinement chapters.

Case Study: Document Automation

A large technology company was looking for new ways of working that would streamline their contracting process to improve efficiency, make the best use of resources, and deliver meaningful impact to the broader business.

The company focused on high-volume, repetitive contracts with a value of less than a million pounds. Over three months, the company rewrote their most-used template, reducing it from 30 to 8 pages (and created a playbook).

The company automated the template and trained the business to use the tool to create the contracts themselves. The results were:

- an empowered business team with a streamlined workflow and without the previous bottlenecks,
- the company reduced the average time to close from months to a matter of days, and
- the in-house legal team could focus on more strategic work.

Case Study 6 - Document Automation

Word extensions

Problem

How can you eliminate the inordinate amount of time spent fiddling with Word documents as part of the contracting process?

Solution

Specialised extensions to Word can significantly improve the speed with which contracts can be reviewed and cost little compared to the time saved. They are also simple to install locally on your computer—a quick, easy win!

Points to consider

Word is a powerful tool, but it is generic and not designed to handle lawyers' issues. This can lead to unacceptable inefficiencies as lawyers struggle with documents and deal with broken formatting. Tools now exist that extend the scope of Word, adding functionality specially for lawyers. As examples of what these tools can do:

- generating issue lists from contracts,
- reversing track changes (so you can quickly and demonstrably reject a change),
- fixing broken documents at the press of a button,
- better document navigation, including being able to see pop-ups with definitions of capitalised terms,
- checking for missing definitions and other issues,
- cleaning up the track changes in documents (e.g., when your colleagues have all added their—conflicting—thoughts using their names), and
- a clause database, allowing lawyers to insert preferred language into contracts and collect useful clauses for the future.

These were the first software tools we built at Radiant Law as they provide such scope for saving time. We approximately halved the time it takes to review a mark-up using the tools we created, which we now license out as RemarkableX[65].

E-signatures

Problem

How can you speed up the signing process and guarantee you get a copy of the final signed agreement?

Solution

E-signatures are now one of the most common contracting technology solutions in use, so if you still haven't implemented them, do it right now.

Points to consider

Most countries have now recognised e-signatures as legally sufficient for most, if not all, commercial contracts (although not always for documents with more formal legal requirements, such as land transfers)[66].

E-signatures offer several advantages over wet ink:

[65] https://radiantlaw.com/lawtech/remarkablex

[66] At their simplest, e-signature systems attach an image of a signature to a document and log the process of how it was signed (typically identifying the signer by a unique link sent to their email address). More complicated signing processes and technology can also be enabled for advanced and qualified electronic signatures under EU law.

- they are far more convenient, improving business satisfaction with the process,
- it is demonstrably faster to obtain signatures this way, reducing the time to close,
- the approvals process can be automated, making it easy to confirm that approvals were given,
- these systems help ensure that contracts are signed (no small feat), and
- they help you find your signed contracts and are also an excellent feed into a contract management system.

E-signature systems can also assist with the pre-signature approvals process, allowing you to send the finalised contract to the approvers (in a pre-set sequence if needed). You can also require them to consent before it is finally signed.

Contract management

Problem

How best to store your contracts and keep track of key dates and actions?

Solution

Put in place the most straightforward contract management system you can and be thoughtful about what data you need to track. In any case, try to avoid throwing away data that you have captured earlier in the process.

Points to consider

One of the most common refrains we hear from contracting teams is that they regularly can't find their signed contracts. Although there are many systems available to help with this (over a hundred), the problem can still arise when you have one. This is because collecting (and managing) contracts is fundamentally a process problem rather than a technology one.

Case Study: The New System

A chief procurement officer was frustrated that their team couldn't identify when the contracts in a particular category would be up for renewal. They installed a contract management system and had a review project carried out to populate the system. The total cost was over £3 million.

To justify the cost, the CPO mandated the collection of many data points for new contracts (not just renewal dates). Uploading a contract was so demanding that many agreements didn't get added by the procurement team. Other teams hadn't been consulted and ignored the system. As the records weren't complete, the procurement team had even more reason to avoid using the system. Renewal dates continued to be checked manually.

Case Study 7 - The New System

I recommend using as simple a system as possible, requiring only a minimal amount of information to be entered and relying on later data extraction exercises to answer future non-standard questions. I will discuss this further in Chapter 8.

For now, the data I would focus on collecting (apart from information on parties, renewal dates, and type) are:

- unusual long-term obligations on you (because you won't comply with them if they aren't made actionable), and

- changes to standard processes, such as approvals (so you know where there will be issues with later bulk updates across your agreements).

Summary

The following are just the base systems you will want to put in place:

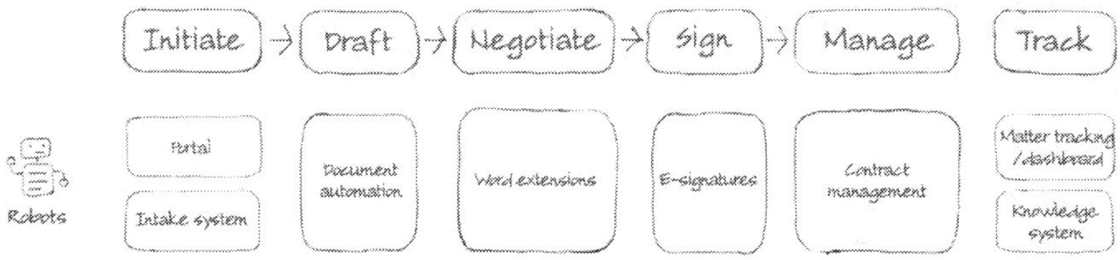

The systems you use will inevitably change over time; what matters is that you focus on adoption at each stage.

With the building blocks of processes, tools, and systems in place, next up is Refinement: the never-ending cycle of improving your contracting process.

Chapter 7 Refinement: Core Principles

For an industry that is so slow to move, the law has plenty of fashions. Year after year, proponents argue that a new approach can be applied and will change everything. Some of these ideas have left little trace (remember Big Data?), while others have helped. Regular practitioners of project management may have been surprised by the sudden enthusiasm for legal project management ("legal" is almost inevitably prepended) when the discipline is old and well understood in other quarters. Still, it's hard to argue that a little project management doesn't go a long way with running legal matters.

These external disciplines are discussed for a while in breathless terms and can be overwhelming to those who don't devote their lives to following the latest trends. Should one use Agile, Lean, Six Sigma, or even Lean Six Sigma? What about design thinking or even visually designed contracts? Where does data analytics, game theory, behavioural economics, or evolutionary psychology fit in? If you don't have a wall covered in Post-it notes, are you doing it all wrong?

How can you make sense of this all and get going? First, it is worth recognising that across many of these disciplines is a common thread: start with the customer's needs. Keep coming back to what matters to the stakeholders in your process ("customer" covers many of those involved or affected) and how you can better deliver it (otherwise known as creating value). Then you will be heading in the right direction. Second, it is better to choose one approach and stick with it than keep chasing novelty. Despite proponents arguing there is only one true way, these disciplines are more like the many faces of a single process improvement god. Third, don't worry too much about purity. If a tool from a different discipline looks helpful, use it.

At Radiant Law, we use two approaches. We use an Agile approach with regular sprints (development periods) for software development. For improving the contracting process itself, we use Lean[67].

As we move now to the third stage of improving your contracting—Refinement—I'm going to explore how to think about quality in contracting, the critical steps in speeding up contracting, how to approach continuous improvement, and finally, how to use data to support your improvement activities. All of these will help you apply the disciplines of process improvement to contracting.

What does "good" look like?

"*There is nothing as practical as a good theory.*" – Kurt Lewin

What is absent from many contracting improvement programmes is a broad understanding of what good looks like. Instead, a particular problem is identified, a (usually overly complex) solution is devised, and off we go. But to evaluate, prioritise, and move forwards thoughtfully, you need a big-picture perspective of where the strengths and weaknesses of your organisation's end-to-end contracting lie and which of them matter. To figure that out, you need a theory of contracting quality[68].

---

[67] For an excellent discussion of how different improvement approaches best apply to the maturity of products, see Simon Wardley's post: https://blog.gardeviance.org/2015/06/why-agile-lean-and-six-sigma-must-die.html. We use Agile with software development because our development work biases towards exploring new areas (we buy standard products where they exist). For contracting improvement, we are in the middle territory of Lean, as described by Wardley, where the process is understood but plenty of waste remains. Perhaps one day we will industrialise contracting to the point where Six Sigma offers the most help.

[68] See Professor Daniel Linna's essay on quality in law for a broader discussion of

Although rare to find in the wild, the basics of a coherent approach to contracting quality are simple: Value lies in the eye of the beholder. There is no objective measure of value; it depends on what's needed by the person being asked. Quality is a function of how well what you deliver meets that person's needs. Therefore, you need to figure out who to ask, establish what they want, and then see how well you are doing against their expectations.

Who are your stakeholders?

Traditionally, if you were a forward-thinking organisation, you would say that the "customer" is the person whose opinion matters. This neat phrasing doesn't solve the problem if you are trying to improve the contracting process within your business:

- There is no one customer within your organisation—all businesses are complex, and there are lots of departments that will benefit in some way from your contracts.

- In this age of environmental, social and governance (ESG) concerns, we are moving to a broader perspective of stakeholders, which includes those participating in delivering the contracts and those impacted by the agreements in other ways.

- Given that the contracting process's purpose is to create sufficient confidence to launch a mutually beneficial commercial relationship, the other party must be a relevant stakeholder, too.

---

this topic:
https://www.legaltechlever.com/wp-content/uploads/sites/151/2020/03/Linna-Evaluating-Legal-Services-Quality-Value-2020-03-12.pdf

Therefore, contenders for your list of stakeholders should include at least the "business", legal, finance, sales, procurement, subject matter experts, the contracting team itself, and the other side.

What matters to your stakeholders?

As well as many potential stakeholders, many things may matter to them. Broadly, however, there are three dimensions to consider:

- **Contracting process**: how well the contracting process itself is running.
- **Contract**: the quality of the final agreement produced by the contracting process.
- **Commercial relationship**: the quality of the relationship created, which builds on both the process and the contract.

Each of these three dimensions has multiple aspects that may be relevant to your stakeholders.

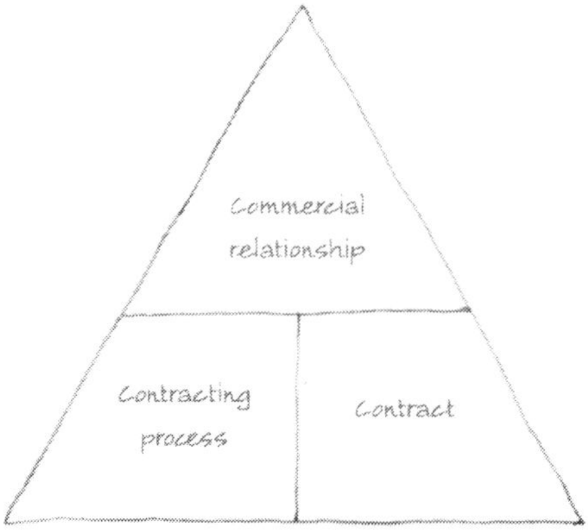

Figure 14 - Aspects of quality in contracting

Contracting process

- **Time to close:** How long does the end-to-end contracting process take[69]? We think this is one of the most important metrics of all.

- **Cost and efficiency**: How much does the contracting process cost for each contract supported? How much time does the team spend on each contract? Ideally, as little as possible, with recognition that it is inefficient to have multiple rounds of negotiations to close minor points.

- **Reliability and responsiveness**: How predictable is the process? How smooth is the process? Does the stakeholder know when they will get a response, and will it be quick? The time for requests to be acknowledged is often one of the most critical metrics for the business. We've identified strong correlations between customer satisfaction and this measure (which preferably should be just a few hours).

- **Assurance**: How good is the work product? Does it follow the playbook? Is advice helpful, clear, and to the point? Are you regularly giving key points away in order to close faster?

- **Empathy**: How did the stakeholder feel during the process? Were they heard? What was the tone of the emails they

[69] There is a balance to be struck here. Closing the wrong deals quickly is unhelpful. Rapidly sending out a piece of work that is incomplete or inaccurate introduces unnecessary risk and may often slow the overall process down. "*Quality is free*," observed Philip Crosby. When I say that the time to close is critical, that assumes a level of quality that is covered in several of the other factors. However, high levels of fiddling with the wording through the drafting and negotiation stages, while common, is not necessarily adding value or meaningful quality.

received? How flexible was the service to accommodate nuances? Did anyone pick up the phone and talk to them?

- **Compliance**: Was the correct process followed? Was the right information sent to the right person?

Contract

- **Clarity**: How understandable and precise is the contract? Does it avoid ambiguity?
- **Length**: How short is the contract? Does it cut to the chase and focus on what matters?[70]
- **Relevance**: How relevant is the contract to what the parties are trying to achieve? Does it cover what matters for what they are buying and selling?
- **Accuracy**: How accurately does the contract reflect the underlying bargain? Are the parties getting what they expected?
- **Usability**: How easy is it to navigate the contract? Can the stakeholder find what they are looking for quickly? Can they be sure that they are reading only relevant part of the contract covering a particular topic?
- **Legal application**: Does the contract appropriately take account of relevant laws to give effect to the parties' intention?

---

[70] Keeping the contract short makes it easier to digest and use. It can also impact time to close. One company tried an experiment of comparing the time to close of one- and two-page NDAs. The one-pager got signed on average in a day while the two-pager took a week.

- **Hygiene**: Is the contract free of typos and formatted consistently? Are the cross-references correct? Interestingly, we occasionally see this metric as the only quality measure in requests for managed legal services. It seems a bit trivial in the context of this list, but I suppose caring about the details is a reasonable proxy, at least to some degree, for caring more widely about the contract. But still, I think we can do better with what we measure.

Commercial relationship

- **Meets commercial objectives**: Has each party achieved its goals for the commercial relationship in the deal? Have the parties expanded the pie and gotten more than they hoped for?

- **Relationship alignment**: Is the relationship set up to succeed? Are the incentives aligned so it is in both parties' interests for the relationship to be long-term and mutually beneficial? Is there a strong likelihood that parties' objectives will be delivered? Is there room for the relationship to grow beyond initial expectations? Is the relationship well-positioned for possible future changes? Has the process created or reduced trust?

- **Risk handling**: Have risks been identified and addressed appropriately? Is the best party (usually the one with the most control of the outcome) bearing each risk? Has each party ensured that the contract does not pose a serious potential threat to them?

- **Profitability**: Is the contract profitable for both parties? For customers, this means that it will deliver more value than the price. For suppliers, it means the price paid exceeds the costs.

With these facets (or at least the ones that most matter to your stakeholders), you can generally measure how contracting is working by comparing the contracting process's performance against your desired standards. You can also measure on a per-contract basis how well the commercial relationship measures up to the ideal and to the contract itself, including how far the agreement deviates from the ideal represented by the standard terms. Finally, you can measure how a contract performs over its term, comparing the actual outcome to expectations.

Don't get bogged down in trying to be too accurate with your measurements. An educated opinion is good enough to get going (and maybe sufficient). Identify your stakeholders, talk them through the different facets described above, and get them to prioritise what is most important to them. Then ask them where the most significant gaps are between what they need and what they perceive is happening. Start your improvement activities by focusing on those gaps.

Closing contracts quicker

If one of the most important metrics is time to close, what improvements will significantly impact speed?

Consider a typical negotiation process. I'm going to break it into blocks of, say, two to four weeks. Some stages will be faster in practice than others on any given deal, but the sequence is inevitable. Although we may all have experienced shorter times for any of these stages, we will also have experienced much longer.

So here is an archetypal negotiation process based on your paper:

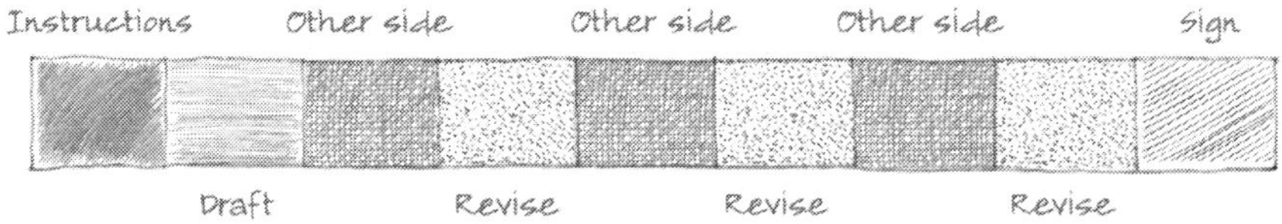

Figure 15 - Contract stages at the beginning

The stages are:

- **Instructions**: getting a clear understanding of what the business is trying to achieve with the contract.

- **Draft**: creating the first draft of the contract and getting the business sign-off.

- **Other side**: the other side reviews the contract and provides a mark-up.

- **Revise**: you, in turn, review the draft and provide your mark-up of the mark-up and so on.

- **Sign**: each party goes through its approval process and signs the agreement.

So, assuming a couple of weeks for each stage, little of which is spent on the deal, that comes to about a four-month end-to-end process. How can we shorten it?

By now, we know the three steps to reduce the timeframes:

- sort out the intake process using a form to elicit clear instructions that don't need further explanation,

- introduce document automation to create the contract in a matter of minutes, and

- use e-signatures to complete approvals and signing in a matter of hours.

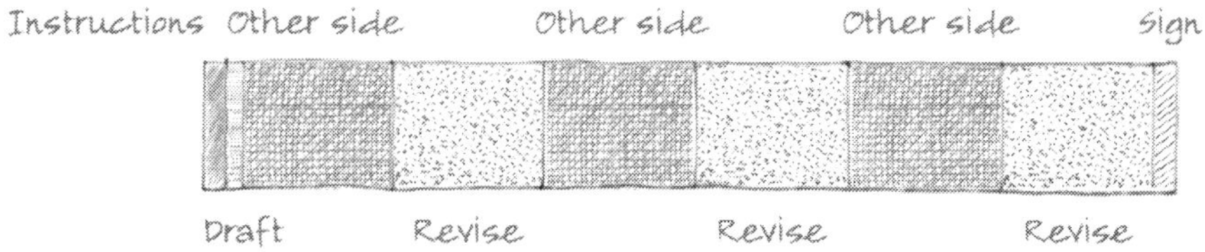

Figure 16 - Contract stages after initial improvements

Already, you've reduced the time to close by 30 per cent. Good work! Next:

- Reduce the time it takes your team to review the contracts from two weeks to half a day. Think that's impossible? I'll explain how we did it at Radiant Law in a moment[71].

That will give you this picture, which is a total reduction of over 60 per cent:

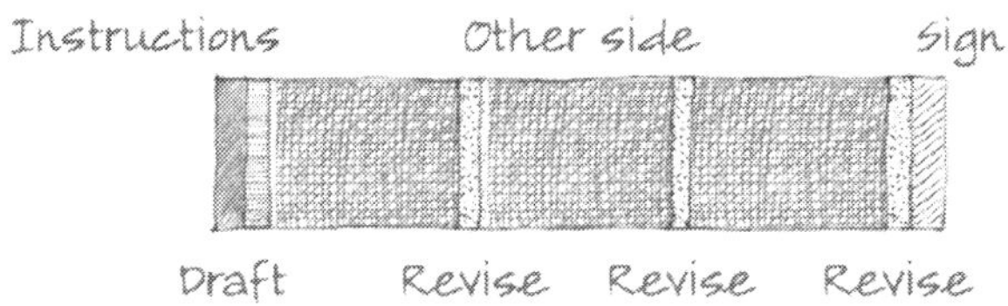

Figure 17 - Contract stages with faster turn-around times

But now it gets tricky. However efficiently you operate, you can't assume that the other side will get quicker[72].

[71] The market standard for managed legal services is currently a two-day turnaround. If you can't meet that internally for simpler standard contracts, it is perhaps time to consider using an external supplier (and focusing the internal team on value-creating strategic activities that cannot be outsourced).

[72] It's true that turning a draft around quickly can influence the other side's

So, the solution to get the next big time saving is to eliminate the other side's need to review the agreement more than once. What you are trying to achieve is a review resulting in no comments raised, and if there are comments, you deal with them effectively in your next round to conclude the deal. Ideally, the process would look like this:

Figure 18 - Contract stages with reasonable terms

And this is why it is so valuable to use reasonable standard terms (as well as ones that are short, clear, relevant, and well designed). Total time saved: about 85 per cent.

Another way of looking at this is to show the value-adding time versus the elapsed time in the initial version. The changes we have made have primarily removed waiting time as well as unnecessary back-and-forth communication:

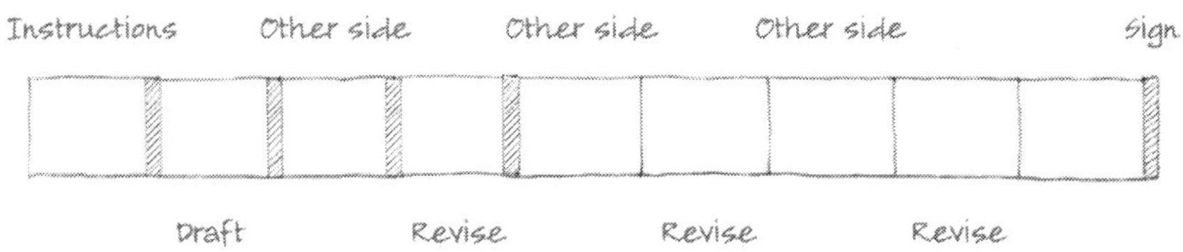

Figure 19 - Contract stages showing value-adding time

turnaround time; if you manage to get it back on the same day, they will remember what is happening and you may find that, in some cases, the contract is, in turn, sent back on the same day. But this effect is the exception in our experience. It's more likely that the agreement will go back on the pile unless it is particularly urgent.

Using data

As you improve your process, you're going to need data to understand what is happening, where to focus your improvement activities, and whether your "improvements" are improving things. Unfortunately, most companies have very little data about their contracting processes, and many don't even know how many contracts they sign each month.

As other departments have created dashboards and started to analyse, with increasing rigour, data related to their part of the business, legal has exhibited jealousy—if not a downright fear that it is falling behind. One of the biggest drivers of new technology projects for contracts is the desire to know when, for example, renewal dates are happening (contract management) or how many contracts are being negotiated (intake systems). The suppliers, noticing this need, have been quick to produce beautiful dashboards.

But the formula seems to be[73]:

1. Buy technology with a dashboard
2. Data!
3. ????
4. Profit!!!

A few conceptual problems are going on here:

- Data by itself doesn't change anything. As Douglas Hubbard points out in his brilliant book *How to Measure Anything*, the point of measuring is to make a good enough decision. You need to start first with the decision you want

[73] From South Park, of course. https://knowyourmeme.com/memes/profit

to make and what data is missing, rather than starting with the data someone else thinks matters.

- The kinds of data you get from a typical system with a dashboard will be initially informative (it would be nice to know how many contracts you are supporting). However, it will become less so over time as you make decisions informed by that data (although keeping your process under control will always be necessary).

- The data that most contracting technology can give you is limited. It may show you what is going on at a high level with your contracts, but over time, you will need granularity.

This doesn't mean that dashboards have no use. Used well, they can help you spot trends over time and exercise control by ensuring that the process is running smoothly[74] and reacting where things aren't working. However, the real value comes from a more purposeful approach to collecting and using data.

Keeping track

One approach to collecting data is to put in place technology using data from document automation, workflow, and the other systems we covered in the Robots stage. Systems-created data can give powerful insights into the contracting process, and we use this regularly at Radiant Law. The problem is that extracting, cleaning, and using this data can often require software development and data analytics skills that are not readily available to the average contracts team.

---

[74] Although that requires the process to be under "statistical control", and most aren't.

As a starting point, informed estimates are not valueless. Polling the team for a quick answer can give you all sorts of insights. However, going beyond this, there is an approach to data that is so simple and effective that it's incredible that it's not more common: paper, pencil, and checkmarks.

If you want to know how many contracts you support a year, don't ask the team how many they support at any point in time. Not only is that not how you count, but it encourages your team not to close their contracts. Instead, track on a piece of paper how many come in over a few weeks or a month. Feels too inaccurate? Keep counting. Want to know what is slowing your team down? Ask them to write down the main obstacles on a piece of paper and then add a checkmark whenever one comes up. Want to know which points you are over-negotiating? Keep a list of clauses and add a checkmark when you negotiate it.

Likewise, by tracking the same issues after you've made a change, you'll be able to see how successful you've been at solving the problem. Overall metrics are essential, but they are often lagging indices. It is hard to show the impact of improvement exercises until much later. It's also hard to connect small changes to overall improvement metrics, meaning the effect could easily get lost in the noise. Using simple tracking exercises that are quick to perform and quick to show improvements allows you to move fast.

When you start measuring, one thing to bear in mind is Goodhart's Law[75]: When a metric becomes a target, it ceases to be a good measure. In other words, teams inevitably start optimising for the

---

[75] Like Campbell's Law, which states that the more a quantitative social indicator is used for social decision-making, the more it will be subject to corruption pressures and the more apt it will be to distort and corrupt the social processes it is intended to monitor.

metric rather than the underlying goal. This phenomenon can lead to counter-productive behaviours[76].

Continuous improvement

I've argued for keeping transformation projects short and sweet. Once you've put the basics in place with the Repeatable and Robots stages, generally, you're going to want to focus on even smaller projects. We've had success with a couple of approaches to maintaining this momentum.

The first is a quarterly cycle of identifying key projects to deliver in consultation with the stakeholders. A quarter of a year works well. You can achieve a surprising amount in a quarter, but it's not so long that the project becomes irrelevant or forgotten. It also allows you to accommodate spikes in volume. We often find they happen at the end of the quarter, and it eventually sinks in with the team that the first month of each quarter is the time to crack on with continuous improvement rather than take a break after the end of the last quarter.

Quarterly projects work well when you know what you need to put in place, but you'll find that change becomes more ambiguous over time, as it is less clear what will work. We've found that the Lean approach of using management challenges works best.

An excellent explanation of this approach can be found in the *Toyota Kata*[77] books by Mike Rothers, which are a good way to introduce Lean to your organisation.

---

[76] To understand how bad this can get, read up on how the British colonial administration in India created a cottage industry of snake breeding when they offered to pay a reward for every cobra caught! https://www.psychologytoday.com/gb/blog/machiavellians-gulling-the-rubes/201610/the-cobra-effect-good-intentions-perverse-outcomes

The katas involve the leadership setting challenges that the organisation is going to meet by a particular date. The team members then need to figure out how to meet the challenge by identifying where they are (the current condition), where the next intermediate goal is (the target condition), and what obstacles stop them from achieving the target condition. As they work on removing the obstacles, the chosen metric will hopefully be improving. Once the target condition is met and becomes the current condition, a new target condition is set until the challenge is completed. This structured and empirical approach to change can lead to dramatic improvements, as shown by the following case study.

---

[77] The term "kata" comes from karate, where it refers to rote exercises for training muscle memory. The purpose of the katas (the improvement kata and the coaching kata) is making scientific thinking a natural instinct. "You can't think your way into right action, but you act your way to right thinking", as Bill Wilson observed.

Case Study: The Turnaround

At Radiant Law, we found that customer satisfaction was heavily driven by how fast we acknowledged the initial request for help from a business user. We were operating on a two-day service level for turning the work itself around (either drafting the contract or dealing with a mark-up back from the other side). We reviewed the time it took to complete the work, and it was clear that it was typically taking less than two hours.

We were comfortably meeting the two-day service level (the average was about a day and a half), but the deal was only being worked on for about 5 per cent of the time that it was with us. So, we set a six-month challenge for the team to reduce turnaround times to 75 per cent completed in half a day (we knew that there would always be outliers that would take longer).

To meet the challenge, the teams on each account tracked the actual performance of turnarounds weekly, reporting through our workflow platform. It turned out that we weren't measuring consistently or accurately enough to see the impact of our improvements, which we fixed with changes to our platform.

Once we had better data, we followed a weekly cycle of setting targets by account and experimenting with removing obstacles. We also redesigned the firm diary so that lawyers had set periods twice a day when they knew they had time to work on deals. By the target date, we had consistently brought down the time taken to turn deals around to meet the "75-per-cent-in-half-a-day" challenge.

This change had some interesting side effects. The team was less stressed because they completed their work on the same day, so they didn't go home at night worrying about what they had to do the next day. We also saw our net promoter score with our business customers rise from about 50 to a perfect 100 for the next three months. As expected, this tailed off a little as the business users got used to the new turnaround times, but it remained over 80, suggesting that speed matters a lot!

Case Study 8 - The Turnaround

Summary

Although there are many process improvement approaches, they all come back to figuring out what matters to your stakeholders, identifying performance gaps, and fixing the issues, ideally with short, quick projects. Try to maintain momentum with steady improvements.

In this chapter, I explained the key steps you need to take to speed up contracting and how to collect data so you can identify key obstacles and confirm that your improvement activities are helping. Finally, I gave two models for improvement: quarterly projects and challenges.

With the basics covered, let's now look at how we can apply these approaches to contracting to solve the most pressing problems.

Chapter 8 Refinement: The Steps

Many of the Refinement activities are ongoing improvements, as there will always be things that can be improved. So, the Refinement stage never ends. The key activities are:

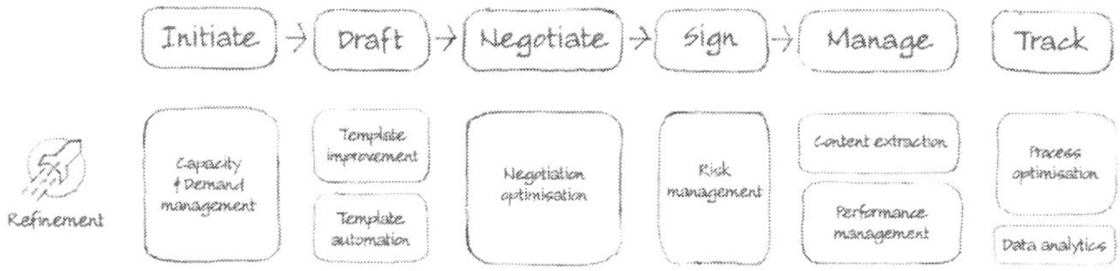

Figure 20 - Refinement stage steps

Talk to your stakeholders to find the gaps between their needs and reality, then start there.

Capacity and demand management

Problem

How to handle spikes in demand for contractual support without slowing everything down?

Solution

Rather than just allowing spikes to overwhelm you, reduce their frequency, severity, and impact and increase your ability to flex with demand.

Points to consider

Spikes in demand regularly swamp most teams, slowing down their ability to turn deals around.

There are several tactics that you can deploy to manage these spikes:

- **Prioritising deals**: We have seen great success in handling bottlenecks by having teams agree with business leads the contracts to prioritise, thus helping meet quarter-end targets.

- **Pricing urgency**: We've also seen teams agree on pricing with their suppliers based on the time taken to turn the work around. The business can choose whether they really need an expedited service.

- **Resource planning**: Get projections from the business on their expected sales and procurement activities and have a single shared plan for the team. Use this to balance resourcing with demand. Keep pushing the planning horizon out. Appoint members of your team to act as business relationship leads with your major customers in the business.

- **Build more scalable resourcing**: Supplement your internal team with third parties who can cost-effectively flex their available resources to handle spikes.

- **Increase self-service**: Run an ongoing programme to increase self-service, including giving business users access to document assembly to create their own simple agreements, as well as playbooks and other resources to handle more contracts.

- **Reduce batch processing**: It's easy to create bottlenecks that lead to unnecessary spikes in volume. These bottlenecks might be draft contracts left to fester on the sales team's desks until the end of the day on Friday or managers needing to give approvals. A quiet word with regular culprits may help; if not, cap the amount of work in progress that will be accepted at one time and make it clear what caused the resulting delays.

- **Reduce the work needed to support an agreement**: Many of this book's suggestions reduce the time and effort required to support contracts. The impact will be increased productivity.

Template improvement and negotiation optimisation

Problem

How to minimise the number of rounds of negotiations?

Solution

In Chapter 7, I explained that reducing the number of rounds of negotiations is critical to reducing the time to close. You need to minimise unnecessary contentious points by refining your templates and playbooks.

Points to consider

People can be just plain difficult. Whether it's a one-off lousy day or a lifetime of grumpiness, you're going to receive unreasonable responses to the most reasonable of terms. In our experience, if you can get this down to less than 10 per cent of the time, so be it.

What's in play is how the other 90 per cent of companies react to your standard terms. To get rid of rounds of negotiations, you need to be sending out agreements and taking negotiation positions that encourage closing rather than trench warfare.

While you will hopefully have made significant progress with this in the Repeatable stage, you're still likely to be surprised at what people misunderstand or react to in practice. That's OK. You just need to keep improving the draft. Similarly, you will have created a playbook in the Repeatable stage, but are the positions you're taking helping to close the contract or extending negotiations unnecessarily?

As you think about how far you want to go with refining your terms and negotiation positions, let's consider the perennial question of whether it's worth throwing in points to concede later.

To answer this, imagine who is going to be reviewing your contract. These days, it's usually an in-house lawyer. This lawyer inevitably has other things to do. Your deal is probably not at the top of their list of priorities, and they're not going to get much recognition for working late. In other words, they have better things to do than have multiple rounds of negotiations. They're going to read your draft (or changes) looking to agree, and the chances are that only when they find a point worth reacting to will they start marking up. So why give them a reason to make changes? Focus instead on knocking all the edges off so that they don't have to change anything. While you're at it, make sure that you have covered sufficiently the regulatory and other issues that subject matter experts on the other side can be so picky about.

And if you need a way of dealing with a negotiator who raises a lot of unreasonable points, don't trade; just say no, explain the issues and hold the line.

With that in mind, here are some points on making ongoing improvements to templates and playbooks:

- **Make regular changes:** Rather than treating playbook or template improvements as a one-off event, make changes at least every few months.

- **Track the frequency of points:** We've built sophisticated software for identifying the issues that come up in negotiations across many drafts, but you don't need this to get started. Just keep a list of the main points and track those that come up. Prioritise the most frequent issues.

- **Removing issues beats collecting fallbacks**: It's better to get rid of a point altogether than have a fallback position in a playbook that you have no problem with conceding. If you can get rid of the issue, then just do it. Both terms and playbooks should be getting shorter as you get smarter.

- **Make it soothing**: A law firm partner I used to work for once said to me: "the purpose of a contract is to send the other side to sleep." It is a little too cynical for my taste, but it makes an essential point about how the wording of a clause can make all the difference between regular fights and nary a mention. If you can't get rid of issues, see if you can make them more palatable. And if the point is a must-have but causes regular fights, then perhaps get ahead of the conversation by sending an explanation with your first draft. While you're at it, try to design the contract to make it as accessible as possible to head off issues.

Template automation

Problem

How to get your contracts automated?

Solution

Set your legal experts to work with an automation expert and get something simple up and running as quickly as possible.

Points to consider

So now you've got a shiny new document automation system courtesy of the Robots stage. Will it become another example of "shelfware", or are you going to use it?

You were probably told the system would make it easy for lawyers to automate their documents. The reality is that few, if any, team members will have the temperament or interest to climb the learning curve, start automating, and then keep going with creating automated templates. Without automated templates, no one can use the system to create new agreements. With that in mind, here are some key questions.

Who is going to do the actual automation?

To automate, you need legal expertise in the subject matter and technical expertise in the system. Ideally, this would be one person. But the reality is that systems are too complex for you to assume that every lawyer will learn to automate their documents.

The best outcome in practice is for a legal expert (who understands enough about the system) to work with a technical expert (who understands enough about contracts). The more legal background the technical expert has, the better, but people combining deep skills in both are unicorns (well, one or two exist).

As an organisation trying to automate your contracts, you have two options. The first is finding someone tech-savvy, interested in learning, and who has the time. Get them to work with the technical expert and learn. This approach can work, but progress may be plodding if your team members do this as a side project. The alternative is to bring in a third party. This will usually be a lot faster, but you need to factor this into your budget and bear in mind that there will be a need for ongoing support.

Which templates should you automate?

There are a couple of approaches to choosing where to start with automating your contracts:

- **Most common first**: Choose the most common contracts that you create as the first to automate. If they are complex, get the team at least partway there with the first draft. If they are simple, aim for completeness (at least for standard options).

- **Champion first:** Your team will inevitably have a range of opinions, from enthusiastic to deeply sceptical, about bringing in new-fangled technologies like document automation. Finding an enthusiast who identifies opportunities for their benefit and then using the results to convince others is a well-tested route to bringing your team along with you. Your champion may be elsewhere in the business, so consider looking beyond the contracting team and think about how you will incentivise them.

How to approach automation?

Let's assume that the automation is going to be done by someone other than the contract expert. Otherwise, the steps below will be more straightforward:

- **Get your template**: You need to have a stable template before you can automate.

- **Flag the clauses that are optional and the variables**: This can be as simple as square bracketing the relevant provisions and adding a comment to show which row of the table below applies. Variables (e.g., party name) just need to be flagged with a comment once.

- **Create a table of questions**: Create a numbered table that sets out the questions and explanatory text (which will be an important part of guiding users and making the system more useable). Use comments or notes in the templates to link the questions to the relevant part of the template.

- **Automate the contract**: With the information above, the person doing the automation should have most of what they need to complete the work, bar some clarifications.

- **Test**: Back to the lawyer to test the template. It's not practical to try every possible combination, but I recommend the following steps:

  - walk through the questions and make sure that the right questions appear and the order is logical,

  - compare the output (with one set of options) against the original template to make sure that it looks right,

  - once you've confirmed that version, create a few other outcomes with the most significant structural differences to the first version, then run comparisons to do a sanity check, and

- test the questions with someone else—ask them to create a document, then watch what they do and where they struggle. However simple you think you've made the questions, this will inevitably throw up surprising issues that you can fix quickly[78].

---

[78] For more on user testing, see Steve Krug's excellent book *Rocket Surgery Made Easy*.

- **Launch:** Once you're happy with the output (and this process should take a week or two, not months), get your users to start using the system and have a single point for them to raise queries and suggestions.

- **Keep iterating (and keep adding templates):** Get into a rhythm of looking at points coming up in negotiations that you can avoid by changing the drafting. Run a campaign to add more documents for automation based on successes to date.

I highly recommend getting a template up and running as quickly as possible and improving it over time. Think of your threshold as the absolute minimum number of questions and options to make the system marginally faster and more practical than manual drafting. Avoid disappearing down rabbit holes trying to cover every possibility. The law of diminishing returns applies, and you will identify the most useful additional options once you start to use the automated template.

One final thought on document automation: it is worth considering whether you always want to have more contracts put in place faster, especially before you put the technology in the hands of your business. For example, are you sure that your organisation will be better off signing more NDAs? As ever, unpack the problem before rushing to automation.

Contract risk management

Problem

How can you appropriately handle the risks associated with your agreement?

Solution

Consider how to manage threats and opportunities across the lifecycle of your contracts. We covered the basics in Chapter 4. Now you need to integrate across the following stages:

- intake, to ensure that you triage matters and identify and address risks early in the process,

- templates, to ensure that the focus is on the essential issues by type of contract and risk handling is balanced,

- negotiations, by refining the playbook to address significant threats appropriately and escalate to senior or specialist input at the right points,

- approvals and signing, with an updated risk review and a process to pass on knowledge of known risks to the contract management team, and

- after signing, so you actively manage the material risks within your control.

Points to consider

The traditional approach to risk management in contracting is to include as many protections as possible for potential threats while jumping on the other side's attempts to transfer risk back. Funnily enough, this mutually-assured destruction approach leads to slow negotiations and frequent stalemates without necessarily focusing on the real issues (as shown by the WorldCC surveys). Uncertainty is an inevitable part of day-to-day business life, and risk allocation is a more complex topic than just avoiding threats at all costs.

Let's define risk widely as significant uncertainty about both threats and opportunities. The goal in handling risk should be to identify those opportunities and threats, reduce uncertainty and apply mitigations where possible, and ensure that the appropriate party carries the consequences (up or down). It is not just about negotiating like Attila the Hun. Importantly, risk-handling doesn't end with signing, and material risks should be actively managed over the term.

I discuss both balancing negotiations and performance management in other sections in this chapter. Here, I'm going to focus on risk analyses.

A formal risk analysis can play an essential role in the process, and you shouldn't wait to start until the end of the deal. As you formalise your approach:

- create a checklist of issues to consider, which should go beyond just "legal" risks to include key commercial points,

- focus in reports on essential topics and avoid minor points drowning them out,

- consider an insurance-style model of *likelihood* times *expected impact* when deciding whether an issue matters (yes, black swan events happen, but does the likelihood justify fighting the point?)[79], and

- try to avoid box-ticking exercises—getting this right requires real thought.

---

[79] Consider your historical experiences when evaluating likelihood and see Douglas Hubbard's book *The Failure of Risk Management* for how to do risk analysis right with a probabilistic model.

Performance management

Problem

How to make sure that you get the hoped-for value from your contracts?

Solution

Identify the critical points for performance management, including risks, put one or more people in charge of managing the contract, and treat your contract as a living document.

Points to consider

Interestingly, commercial contracts work, although they are rarely litigated. Parties seem to moderate their behaviours despite the low risk of being sued (it's such an expensive remedy that it's seldom worth pursuing) and generally comply with their obligations (though there are legions of minor technical breaches), so contracts kind of work[80].

What's also interesting is the study by WorldCC mentioned in Chapter 1, which suggests that the bottom line of companies is, on average, over 9 per cent lower than it might be because of contract value leakage. Bad contracts rarely explode; instead, they may slowly bleed value due to poor scoping and pricing or drift from the original intentions.

Perfect value maximisation may never really be achievable. Still, I'm sure that we can always be better at managing and growing our

---

[80] An explanation for this perhaps lies in Professor Macneil's identification of social norms as a crucial part of the framework within which contracts operate.

commercial relationships[81]. We can certainly be better at managing contractual performance.

Rather than assuming that the things you care about in the contract will happen, you should actively manage the material opportunities and threats and track outcomes against initial expectations.

Pragmatically, it is best to focus on material agreements. Your process should include:

- identifying one or more people to take responsibility for managing the contract,
- a hand-over process after signature to pass the main identified risks to the contract owners (this is where it often goes wrong), and
- an oversight and reporting process.

You can track points in a spreadsheet in the first instance, but some contract management systems specialise in supporting more active management of large deals.

You also need to manage the relationship itself. This entails more than mechanically attending governance meetings. It means getting ahead of nagging issues, identifying ways to improve both parties' outcomes, and working together to find opportunities to grow.

As you do this, it would help if you found a middle path between whacking your partner over the head with the contract and leaving it in a drawer. Avoid treating the contract as frozen in aspic for all time. It should move from a baseline for the start of the relationship

[81] 20 percent of companies are actively managing their commercial contracts, according to the Radiant Law Contract Scorecard.

to an ongoing record of the current deal, meaning that you continue to update it as a living document.

As you update your contracts, you'll find that keeping a final Word version from the point of signature is invaluable. You will also find that amending a contract with separate amendments, rather than continuing to update the final Word version, will quickly become unworkable.

Content extraction and contract data

Problem

How to store data relating to your contracts?

Solution

Design a data structure that makes sense, keeps data points from throughout the contracting process and the final versions of the contract, and minimises metadata.

Points to consider

I mentioned in Chapter 6 that finding your contracts was a process problem rather than a technical one. A simple solution to finding your contracts is to set up an email address to send them to after signature. If you can't make that work, a contract management system won't solve your problem finding agreements. E-signature systems help, but they too have to be used.

In the case study of the contract management system, we saw that requiring lots of data to be entered will probably reduce use. As tempting as it may be to capture everything, it will likely be counter-productive. So, keep the data fields to a minimum, but don't throw away any data you have. For the data to help, you will need a sensible way of storing it, so it's worth taking the time to think through the data structure. As noted in the performance management section, keep the final Word version. It will make future amendments much easier.

Not capturing every data point may appear unambitious, but future questions are surprisingly unpredictable, however much data you capture. Better to avoid manual extraction until it is needed. AI extraction is only going to get better, so future exercises will become easier with time.

Summary

Congratulations, you've made it through all the steps. It may feel like there is an insurmountable amount of work involved, but it can be done steadily and in bite-sized chunks. We've covered all of these steps in two chapters:

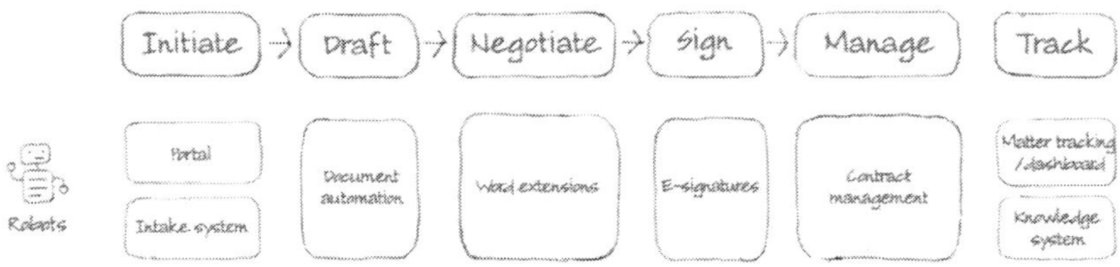

Of course, contracting is not staying still. In the next chapter, I will cover where the future of contracting seems to be heading. Please don't use future possibilities as an excuse to skip the steps in this book. All of these will still hold, and the future of contracting needs to be built on solid basics.

Chapter 9 The Future of Contracting

I am wary of futuristic takes on contracting, as the problems we face come from not doing the basics, and many of the solutions we need are available here and now. But if I don't mention the blockchain, smart contracts and AI, then at least some readers will feel cheated, and how can I resist doing a drive-by on these topics? So here goes.

The blockchain continues to be a solution looking for a problem, and despite all the hype to date, it has failed to demonstrate much value in the world of contracting that cannot be delivered using far simpler solutions. The problems we have are as mundane as not finding contracts, rather than fraud (and there are more straightforward ways of solving a fraud problem without needing the blockchain). Therefore, I predict that there will not be far-reaching use of blockchain technology in commercial contracting within the next thirty years (my working horizon). Still, we will continue to be nagged by the sellers of snake oil.

I also predict that smart contracts (that is, contracts running as code on a blockchain as opposed to computable contracts, which I'll discuss below) will fail to get widespread traction for two reasons:

- First, smart contracts will likely turn out to have few practical use cases, given their limited ability to affect the real world. Yes, they can release cryptocurrency funds from escrow, but has anyone checked with a CFO about the desirability of locking up material sums in escrow? If the program can't control the world, then the smart contract's core point is defeated.

- Second, there are fundamental problems with applying computational reasoning to a messy world.[82]

Much of the world will continue to be eaten by software, as noted by Silicon Valley supremo Marc Andreessen. Some actions previously controlled by contracts will instead be controlled by code. Still, I don't expect smart contracts to play a significant role.

Finally, I explained previously the limited role that AI currently plays in contracting. I expect that we will get better at recognising clause types and using this to give hints to reviewers of agreements. I also hope that a breakthrough will allow computers to reason about clauses' meaning, but it will require a different approach to the technologies currently being used[83]. I don't expect the impact to be particularly dramatic. We will still have had to do the basics set out in this book (good luck with getting a computer to interpret a contract you can't find!), and there will be more mileage in writing clear contracts than in waiting for a machine to decipher legalese.

If the blockchain, smart contracts, and AI won't significantly impact contracting, what will be different? If past performance is anything to go by, progress will probably continue to be slow, but there are three themes that I hope to see more of, above and beyond a wider adoption of the RADICAL approach to contracting. Those three themes are the human dimension, abstraction, and computability.

---

[82] Sean McGrath has written a brilliant seventeen-part series on the computational challenges that come from the inherent ambiguities in law and contracts. All of it is worth reading, although parts 16 and 17 particularly focus on smart contracts. https://seanmcgrath.blogspot.com/2017/03/what-is-law-part-1.html.

[83] If you want to understand more about the limits of the current approaches to AI, it is worth reading Gary Marcus's works:
https://en.wikipedia.org/wiki/Gary_Marcus

It's all about humans

In all the talk of applying technology to contracting, it's easy to forget that this is about relationships, even if they are commercial relationships, and therefore about humans. Ultimately, relationships are between people, and it is people who will decide whether to invest in one or let it wither. You must get people to agree with you and to value what you offer. It is people who experience the contracting process that you create, not machines. The endgame should not be fully automated trading systems but humans building relationships with other humans to add value for humanity[84].

As we enthuse about innovation and increasing automation, let's spare a thought for the user experience. We need to be designing processes that are delightful for all the participants, including the other side, and that embrace the contracting function's role in marketing your company. Remember that humans don't create relationships with technology[85].

Of course, we don't need to wait for an automated future to care about the contracting experience. Right now, too many parties get to experience "computer says no" through monolithic standard terms, unreasonable contracting policies, and teams who refuse to engage with the other side, all of which boils down to corporate-scale bloody-mindedness.

---

[84] I mentioned "relational contracting" earlier—the furthest end of the transactions-relationships spectrum. This approach focuses on building early trust and collaboration through an exploratory model of negotiation that emphasises growing the pie and adapting to changing circumstances. I have included an article in the Reading List at the end of this book, if you are interested in learning more.

[85] With the possible exception of Apple's customers.

Abstraction

In computer science, "abstraction" is used to hide the less important details to reduce complexity. Over time, programmers have created "higher level" programming languages and tools that let them focus on business logic, ignoring how the computer works underneath. As abstraction has increased over time, programming has become much faster and programmers more productive[86].

We need a similar approach in contracting. We spend too much time in the weeds, forcing business users to engage with impenetrable contracts that obfuscate the essential points. Those of us who are experts in the law have created a dependency that means we have to be involved and consulted to make sense of contracts and implement them safely.

While there will always be a need for specialist advice, I expect to see systems emerge that empower business users to run most, if not all, of the contracting process themselves. These systems will provide guidance and guardrails to allow the users to focus safely on the business issues and not on the contractual language itself. The challenge with these systems is that they typically require both parties to change their behaviours and drop Word and email, so we can safely assume that this won't happen any time soon. I expect the parties will need to move to a neutral third-party platform that allows them to choose between negotiation options to minimise the need for free-form drafting. And if you can do this, then you can move to data-centric contracts.

[86] It also means that software typically runs slower but increasing computing power has more than made up for this.

Data-centric and computable contracts

Contracting is currently overwhelmingly document-centric. Even if it never gets printed out, a typical contract is made up of one or more documents with little, if any, structure to the critical data points. Departments must revisit agreements regularly and spend fortunes reviewing them to deal with the latest regulatory change.

This is hardly practical, and as suggested in the last chapter, a good start would be to stop throwing data away. But consider this thought experiment: if you were to build a sufficiently complex document automation template that covered the majority of the negotiation points that arise in practice[87] (a large but still finite set of options), then the outcome of any negotiation could be represented mostly, if not totally, as data—in particular, the options selected. If you could store that data as a representation of the contract, then you would just need to interrogate that data to answer questions about what is lurking in your contract portfolio. This is what I mean by data-centric contracting.

A data-centric approach would still require you to read the contract's language to answer questions. Some of these questions (often relating to financial provisions) might best be answered by representing the agreed position not just as data but modelled as actual code. Not all provisions in an agreement lend themselves to being encoded, and with this approach, there would still need to be a human-readable version of the deal. The advantage of code is that the contract (or rather the coded representation) would answer questions about different scenarios, allowing sophisticated

[87] Oliver Hart and Bengt Holmström won the Nobel Prize for Economics in 2016 for their theory of incomplete contracts. They rightly note that a contract cannot cover all contingencies. That doesn't mean that a system can't handle the most common points that come up in negotiations.

modelling across portfolios. We call these contracts computable or Ricardian agreements, not to be confused with the smart contracts loved by blockchain-boosters, where the contract is the code (with all the problems I highlight above).

Computable contracts are an attractive concept for financial institutions, which spend significant resources on modelling derivatives and other financial instruments and have led the way in developing this approach. At least one of the leading insurance and asset management groups have a board-backed initiative to make their core products computable. I expect that this will spread in the future.

To implement computable contracts, you will need most of this book's steps and you'll have to adopt the abstraction approach[88]. As warned early on in the no-silver-bullets section, completeness will also be a challenge. It won't happen soon, but it will put the power back in the end-user's hands, so I think it's worth pursuing[89].

Summary

Although there is much that lawyers bring to the contracting process, I am a firm believer in the potential of empowering our end-users to do more, with lawyers (leveraging technology) focusing on the more complex transactions and creating the systems that will

---

[88] Because negotiations will need to be limited to predetermined options as no one is going to want to rewrite code as part of a negotiation.

[89] The observant reader will note that I have raised a couple of serious objections in this book to such a system. It would need to support discussions between humans since relationships are ultimately between humans, and it assumes that for at least some types of deals, the system could be complete enough to be practical. It would also have to be built on commonly accepted terms, which are still the exception. I think it's possible, but difficult.

empower the business. As we do this, it will be a terrible mistake if we focus on the automation and not the relationships we are trying to create. Relationships are ultimately between humans, so our future systems need to create spaces for better, more informed communication, not more opportunities for computers to say no. I'm optimistic, but there is plenty to do first to get the basics in place.

Conclusion

And that's it! Not everything there is to know about fixing your contracting, of course, but a framework to help you prioritise, focus on what matters, and get going.

Reading about it is the easy part; doing it takes time. As you get started, try to tame your inner perfectionist and use the "good enough for now" test. You're not going to make constant progress and you will be overwhelmed at times with the day-to-day work, but that's OK. Come back to it when you're ready, and know that there is help at hand if you need it. And remember, as you put the pieces in place, the day-to-day work will get easier.

To be successful, you will need to bring your team and then the broader business on the journey to adopt these new ways of working. But the whole team doesn't have to change at once. You can start with the early adopters and sweep up the laggards later. For this to work, though, you will need management support for the changes and a more balanced approach between risk and speed. Start in one part of your organisation, show the benefits, and bring the others with you.

One reviewer of this book wondered if most teams will do something and then stall. Perhaps, but it doesn't have to be that way. The three things that have helped us keep going are:

- **Leadership attention**: Ongoing change requires consistent attention from the top that recognises that there will be times when everyone is too busy but keeps applying (reasonable) pressure.

- **Time**: Leaders also need to provide support. Most importantly, continuous improvement is real work and will take time. Give the team that time. Otherwise, change won't happen.

- **Cadence**: Create a rhythm of regular meetings, challenges and reporting back. After a while, the team will just accept change as part of business-as-usual!

Once the team has adopted this approach as a habit, you'll wonder how you ever managed it before.

About Radiant Law

Radiant Law is an award-winning UK law firm with teams in London, Cape Town, and Toronto helping some of the world's largest companies with their commercial contracts. We combine fixed pricing (to give our clients price certainty and align interests), legal judgement, design, data analysis, Lean, and technology to help our clients fix their contracting problems. We are also a certified B Corp, a new kind of business that balance purpose with profit to build an inclusive and sustainable economy that works for everyone.

Radiant Law has won the FT Innovative Lawyers' award for Pioneer Law Firm of the Year and the Managing Partners Forum's Mould-Breaking Firm of the Year. We are acknowledged as one of the global leaders of a new type of law firm, appearing in books such as *Tomorrowland: Scenarios for Law Firms Beyond the Horizon* (Bruce McEwan, 2017), *Tomorrow's Lawyers: An Introduction to Your Future* (Richard Susskind, 2013), *The Rise of Legal Outsourcing: Risk and Opportunity* (Mary Lacity et al., 2014) and *The Great Legal Reformation: Notes from the Field* (Mitch Kowalski, 2017).

How we help our clients:

Radiant Run

We provide end-to-end fixed-price managed legal services to support high volumes of day-to-day contracts, from intake and triage to drafting, negotiation, and the approvals process.

Projects

We deliver large-scale contract review and remediation projects, including support for regulatory changes to fix existing commercial contracts or transfer them as part of a business sale or outsourcing.

Optimisation

We deliver quick projects to improve contracting processes, such as redrafting templates, creating playbooks, automating documents, and introducing other technology. We also provide consulting services to help find innovative approaches to complex challenges.

Deals

We provide fixed-price support for large outsourcing, technology, and other commercial contracts for both customers and suppliers.

Legal Tech

We build and licence legal tech, including RemarkableX, our Word extensions, and help clients select and implement third-party products.

Next steps

There are several resources to help you get going on your contracting improvement journey:

Contracting Scorecard

The Radiant Law Contracting Scorecard helps you measure where you are on the contracting journey and what to prioritise next. The Contracting Scorecard is free to use, and you will receive a customised report.

Visit: www.radiantlaw.com/scorecard

Contracting Workshops

We hold regular free live workshops explaining RADICAL contracting and the 3Rs improvement approach.

Visit: www.radiantlaw.com/workshop

Contracting Guides

We have published multiple free guides and resources for improving the contracting process.

Visit: www.radiantlaw.com/resources

Get in touch

I wish you the best of luck as you tackle your contracting process. I would love to hear how you do, and if you ever want to ask questions or share experiences, you can find me here:

Email: alex.hamilton@radiantlaw.com

Twitter: @alexhamiltonrad

LinkedIn: linkedin.com/in/alexhamilton/

Web: radiantlaw.com

The Author

Alex Hamilton

Alex trained as a lawyer, working at Norton Rose and Shaw Pittman (now Pillsbury Winthrop Shaw Pittman) before making partner at the global US firm Latham & Watkins, where he specialised in outsourcing and complex technology deals and co-chaired the global Technology Transactions Group. After a Jerry Maguire-like moment where he wrote a mission statement (not a memo) to the executive committee in 2009 calling for more innovation[90], he left to found Radiant Law in 2011.

Alex has worked in London and New York and is qualified to practice English and New York law. He has negotiated some of the largest outsourcing deals worldwide and has led seven projects ranked in the FT Innovative Lawyers awards. He is a fellow of the College of Law Practice Management and was a finalist for the FT's Legal Innovator of the Year Award. Alex is also a regular public speaker about contracting improvements, legal tech, and the changing legal industry and has been known to share one or two opinions on these topics on Twitter.

Alex is now the CEO of Radiant Law, which means that he doesn't do many deals any longer but does get to lead a team of lawyers, developers, engineers, data analysts, and designers in reinventing legal services. This has turned out to be even more fun.

[90] https://alexhamiltonrad.tumblr.com/post/78751332144/innovation-opportunities-executive-summary

Acknowledgements

Many people helped make this book possible. For starters, our clients who backed us and the Radiant Law team who figured out how to make contracting fly, one contract at a time. It's been a hell of a journey working with you all over the past ten years. Greg Tufnell and Serena Wallace-Turner, without whom Radiant Law would have been just another also-ran. All the people who so generously reviewed and commented on this book—the wrong-headed opinions and mistakes remain mine, the credit for the smarter points is all theirs: Ken Adams, Paul Boyle, Peter Carayiannis, Martin Clausen, Professor Norman Faull, Ken Grady, Sol Irvine, Professor Richard Moorhead, Denis Potemkin, Ian Teague, and Duc Trang. World Commerce and Contracting, who led the way in applying rigour and empiricism to contracting. Vita Hamilton, Maeve MacGlinchey, Verity Ridgman, and Susan Ryan for their brutally tough editing. Bill Bonney of Last Mile Publishing, Theo Hamilton, Tim Hamilton, Dawn Hapgood, Nicola Lyons, and Mykola Shelepa for their excellent eyes as we agonised over the artwork and layout. It's good to be surrounded by people who care so much about the details. And finally, Nonku Nyathi for her abiding support and patience as I paced up and down, trying to get the ideas straight in my head.

Thank you all.

Further Reading

Ken Adams. *A Manual of Style for Contract Drafting*
4th ed, American Bar Association, 2017
The definitive guide to drafting clearer contracts.

Niklas Modig and Pär Åhlström. *This is Lean*
Rheologica Publishing, 2012
A great introduction to Lean principles, underlining that it is more than a set of tools.

Gerald Langley, Ronald Moen, Kevin Nolan, Thomas Nolan, Clifford Norman, Lloyd Provost. *The Improvement Guide*
2nd ed, Jossey-Bass, 2009
A comprehensive guide to process improvement, following the Lean approach.

Douglas Hubbard. *How to Measure Anything*
3rd ed, Wiley, 2014
A practical primer on how to make better decisions and apply statistics to your data.

Douglas Hubbard. *The Failure of Risk Management*
2nd ed, Wiley, 2020
An introduction to how to do risk management right.

Mike Rother. *Toyota Kata*
(McGraw-Hill, 2009)
The introduction to the Toyota Kata, an exercise for building scientific thinking in your team.

Marc Stickdorn, Markus Edgar Hormess, Adam Lawrence, Jakob Schneider.
This is Service Design Thinking
BIS Publishers, 2014

This is Service Design Doing
O'Reilly Media, 2016
Introduced the world to service design thinking (and doing).

Steve Krug.
Don't Make Me Think, Revisited
3rd ed, New Riders, 2014

Rocket Surgery Made Easy
New Riders, 2009
Written originally for website user testing, the principles hold for any form or system you ask end-users to adopt.

Lou Downe. *Good Services*
BIS Publishers, 2020
A practical guide to the fundamental principles for improving (particularly online) services.

W. Edwards Deming. *Out of the Crisis*
MIT Press, 1982
A guide to how organisations (and their approach to systems and processes) need to be rethought.

Roger Fisher and William Ury
Getting to Yes
3rd ed, Baker and Taylor, 2011

Getting Past No
Random House, 1992
The original guides to principle-led negotiations.

Atul Gawande. *The Checklist Manifesto*
Profile, 2011
A terrific introduction to why checklists matter and why professionals are dangerous without them.

Eliyahu Goldratt. *The Goal*
3rd ed, Routledge, 2004
The introduction to the theory of constraints, which is a core underpinning to improving processes.

David Frydlinger, Oliver Hart and Kate Vitasek
A New Approach to Contracts
Harvard Business Review, September 2019
An introduction to relational contracting.

James Womack and Daniel Jones
Lean Thinking
Simon & Schuster, 2003

Lean Solutions
Simon & Schuster, 2005
Two books focused on Lean, including banishing waste and viewing producers and customers as one system. Lean Solutions is more services focused.

Duc V. Trang. *Architecture of Deals*
Academy Publishing, 2019

Introduces a framework for applying core economic concepts to transactions, explaining some important mechanisms in deals.

Caroline Jarrett and Gerry Gaffney. *Forms that Work*
Morgan Kaufmann, 2008
A practical guide to making usable forms that will transform how you think about collecting information.

Art Smalley. *Four Types of Problems*
Lean Enterprise Institute Inc, 2019
How to apply Lean methodologies to solving different types of problems.

Jeffrey K. Liker and Karyn Ross. *The Toyota Way to Service Excellence: Lean Transformations in Service Organizations*
McGraw-Hill Education, 2016
Applying Lean to service organisations.

Index

Index

Illustrations

List of Case Studies

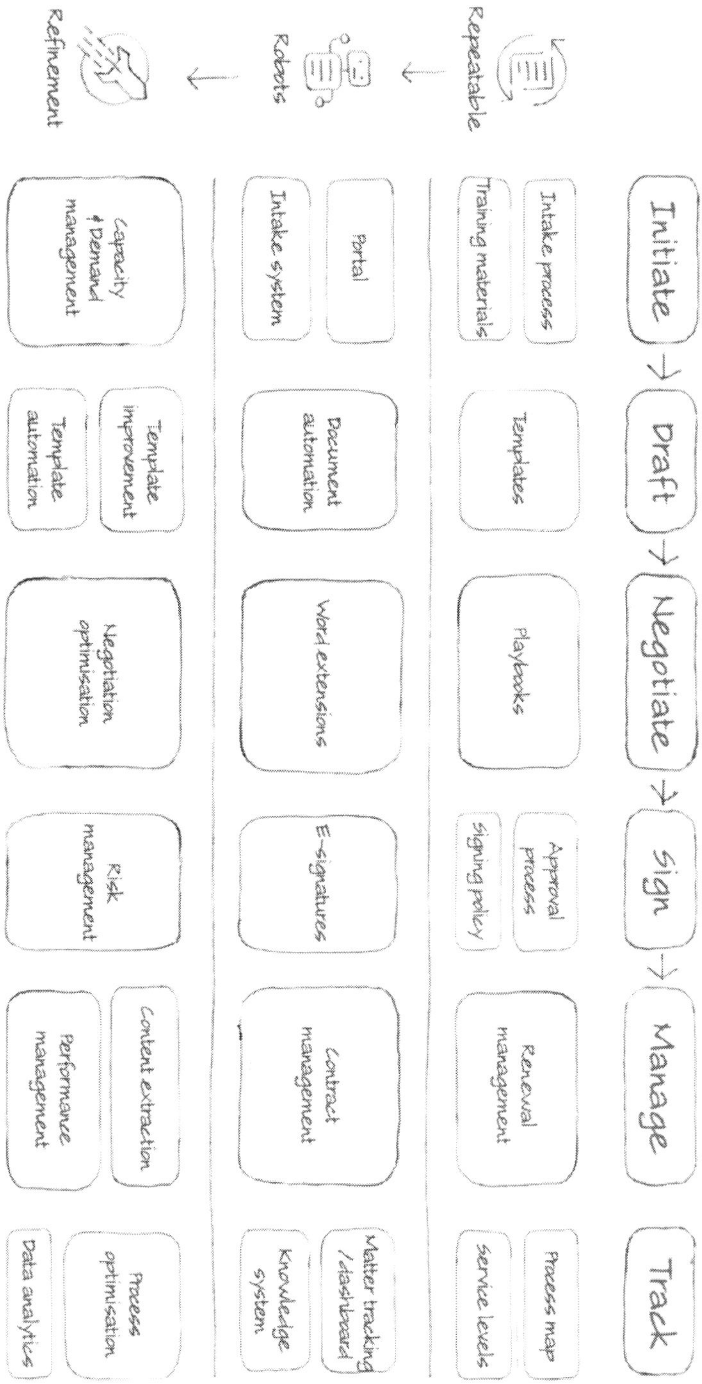
Initiate
Draft
Negotiate
Sign
Manage
Track
Repeatable
Intake process
Training materials
Templates
Playbooks
Approval process
Signing policy
Renewal management
Process map
Service levels
Robots
Portal
Intake system
Document automation
Word extensions
E-signatures
Contract management
Matter tracking / dashboard
Knowledge system
Refinement
Capacity & Demand management
Template improvement
Template automation
Negotiation optimisation
Risk management
Content extraction
Performance management
Process optimisation
Data analytics

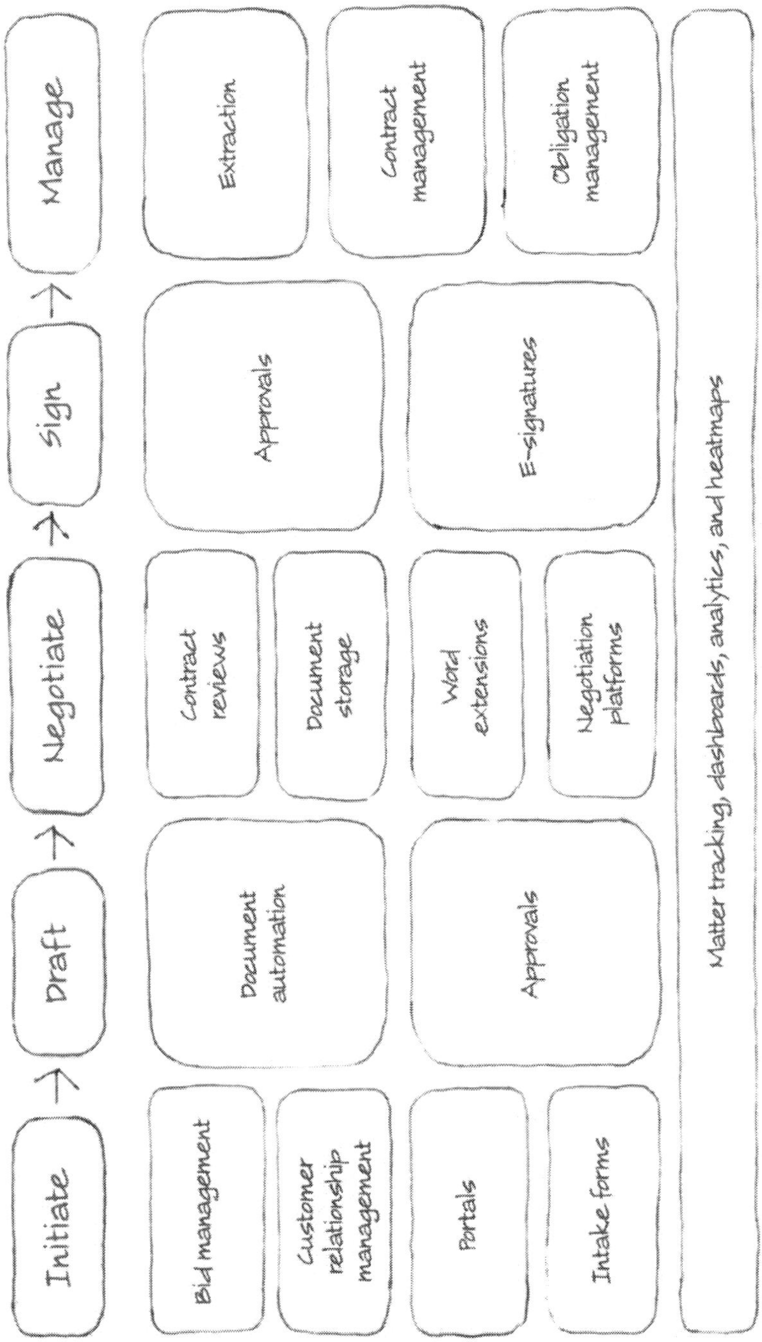
Initiate
Draft
Negotiate
Sign
Manage
Bid management
Customer relationship management
Portals
Intake forms
Document automation
Approvals
Contract reviews
Document storage
Word extensions
Negotiation platforms
Approvals
E-signatures
Extraction
Contract management
Obligation management
Matter tracking, dashboards, analytics, and heatmaps

Printed in Great Britain
by Amazon

29851292R00101